Album of Astronomy

Michael Martins

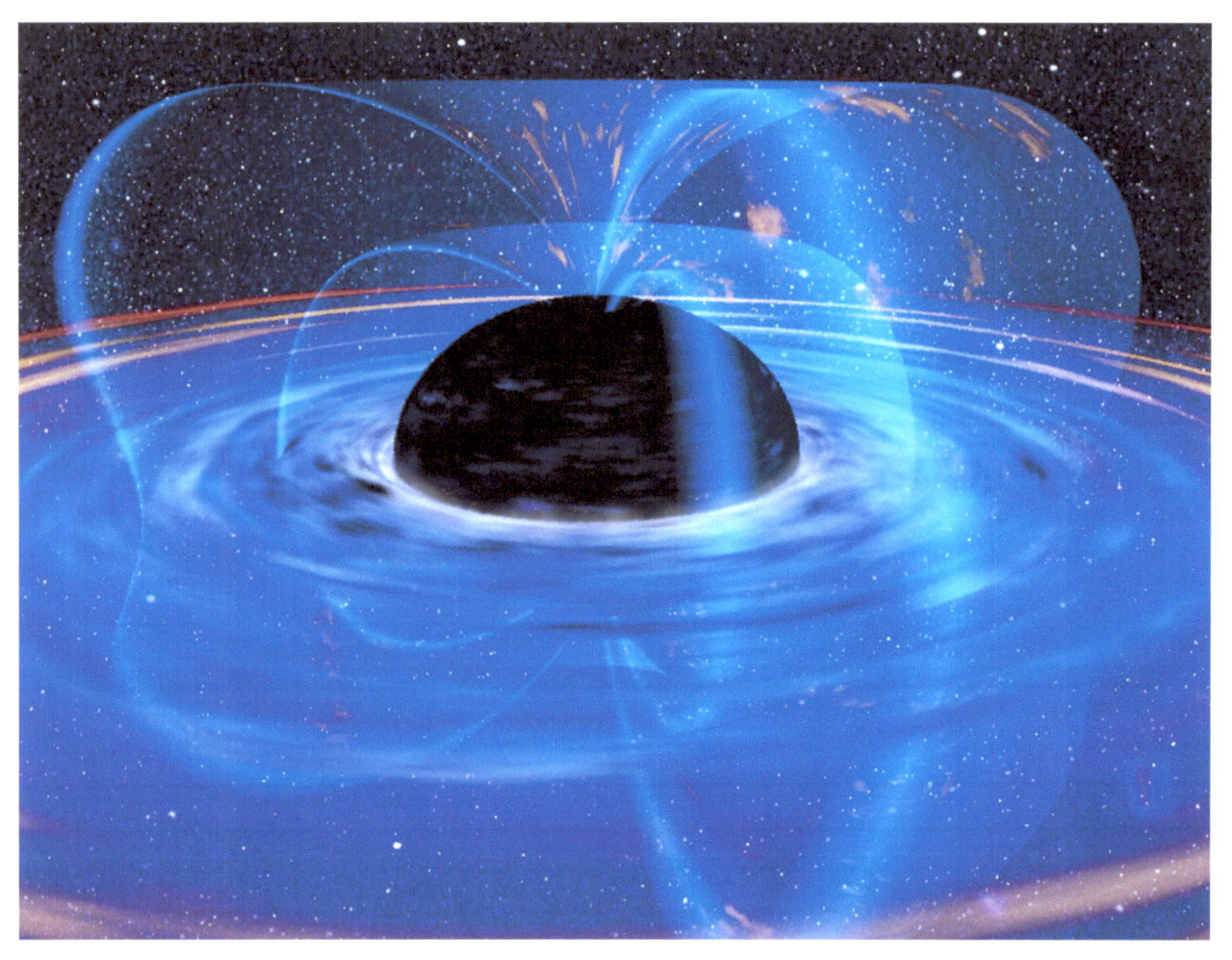

Begin of Journey

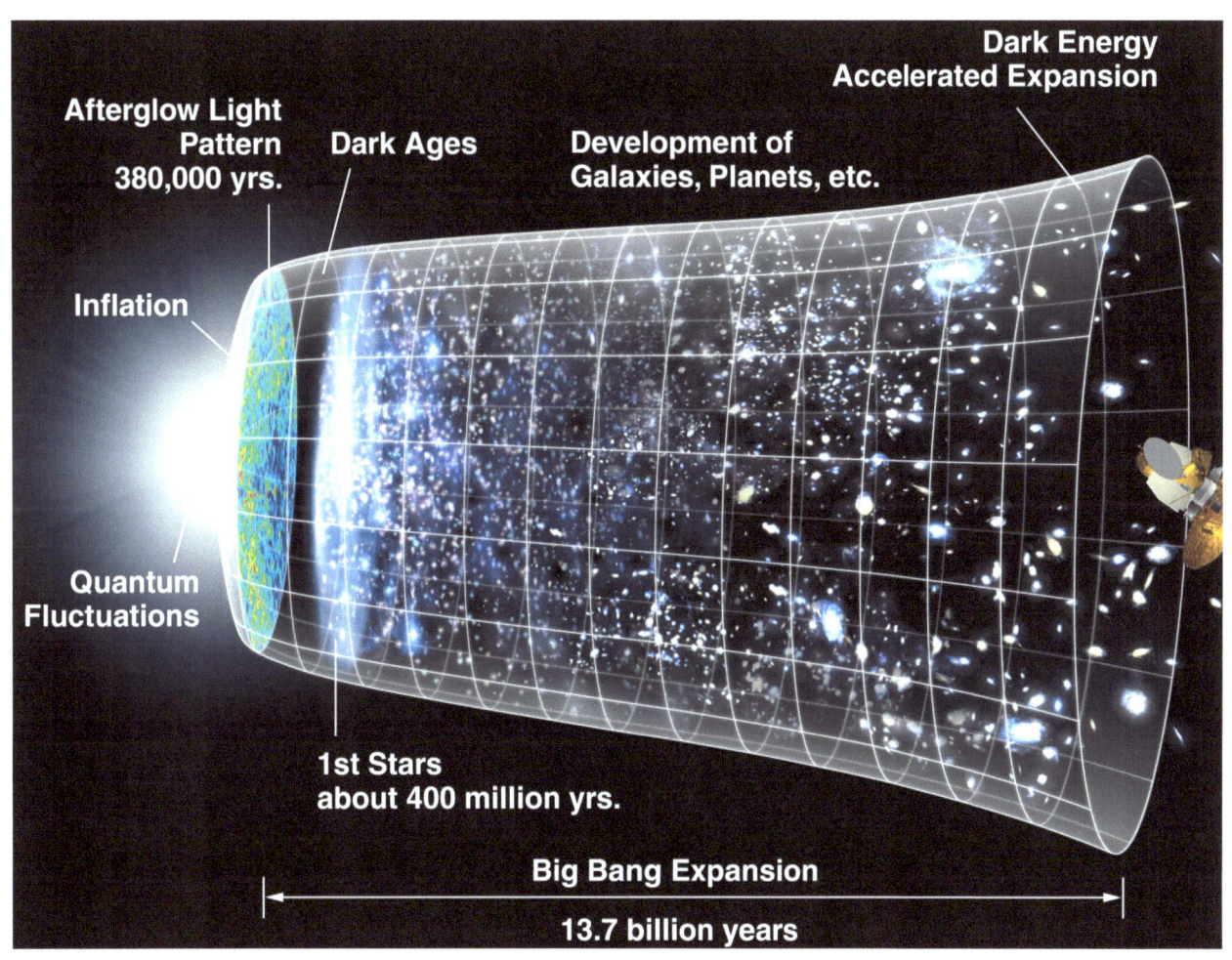

Ignition of
Space and Time
Huge amounts of energy
through a pinhole

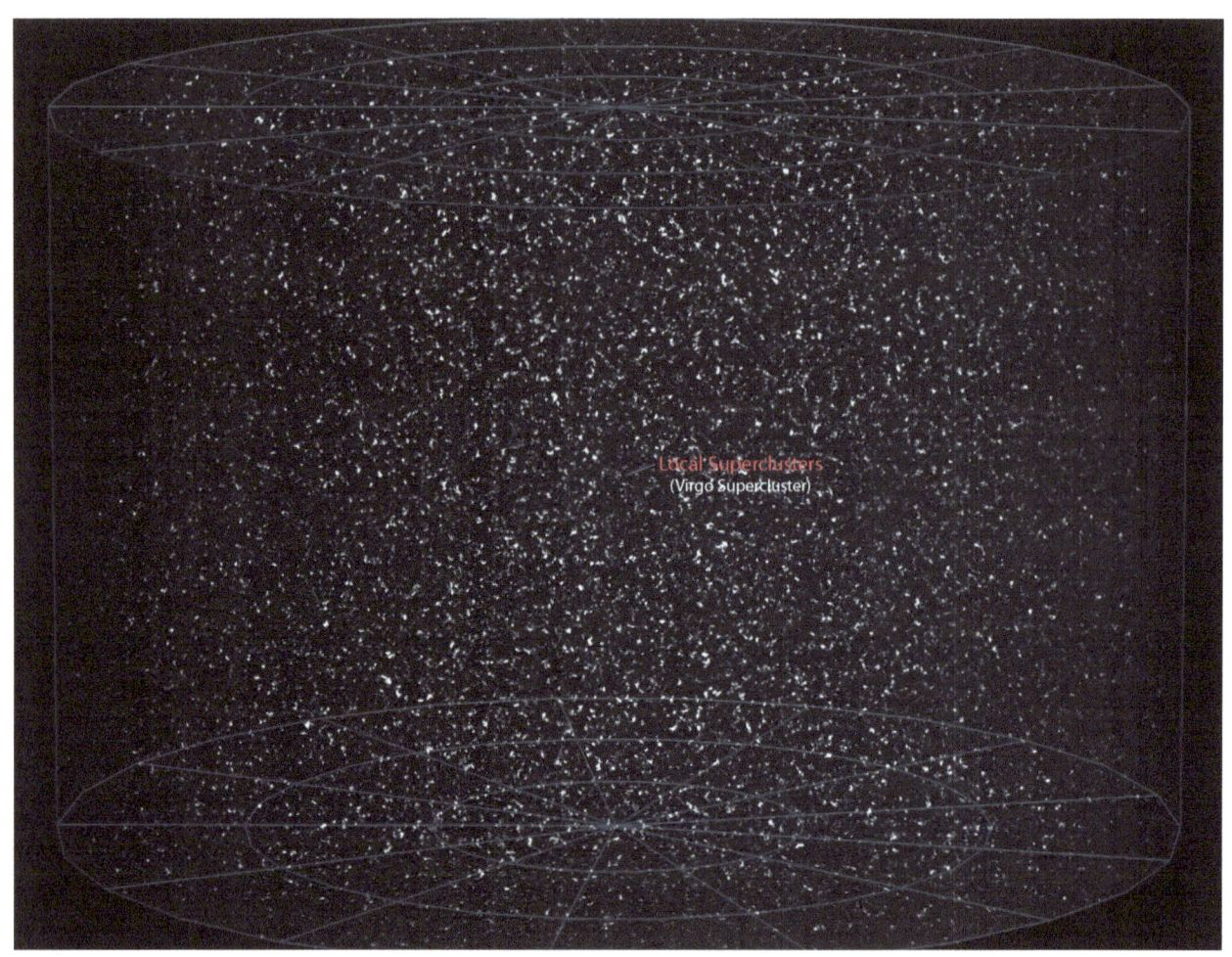

Local Superclusters
(Virgo Supercluster)

Uni-Verse

Stars in all directions

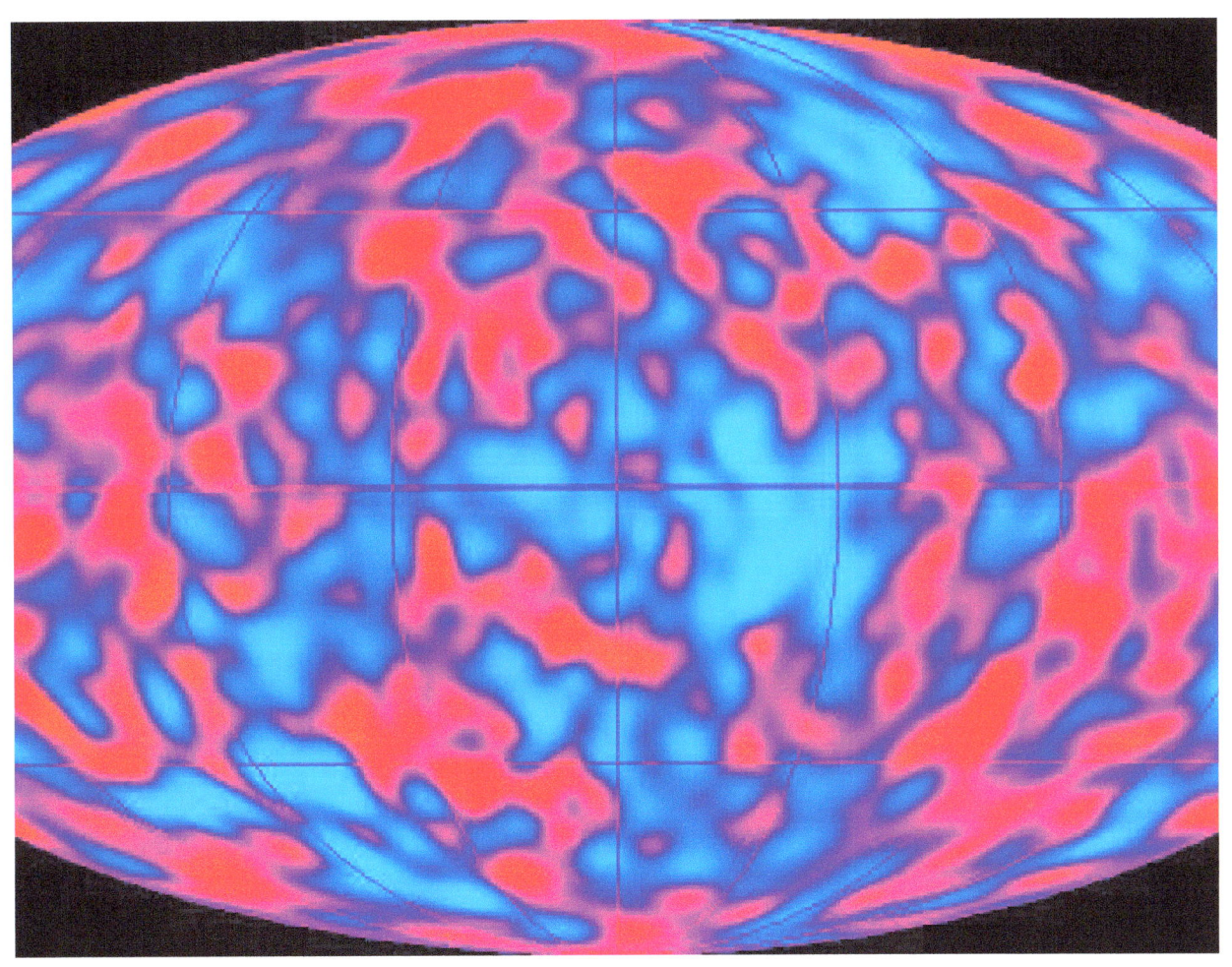

Afterglow
Remnants of the
Big Bang as radiation

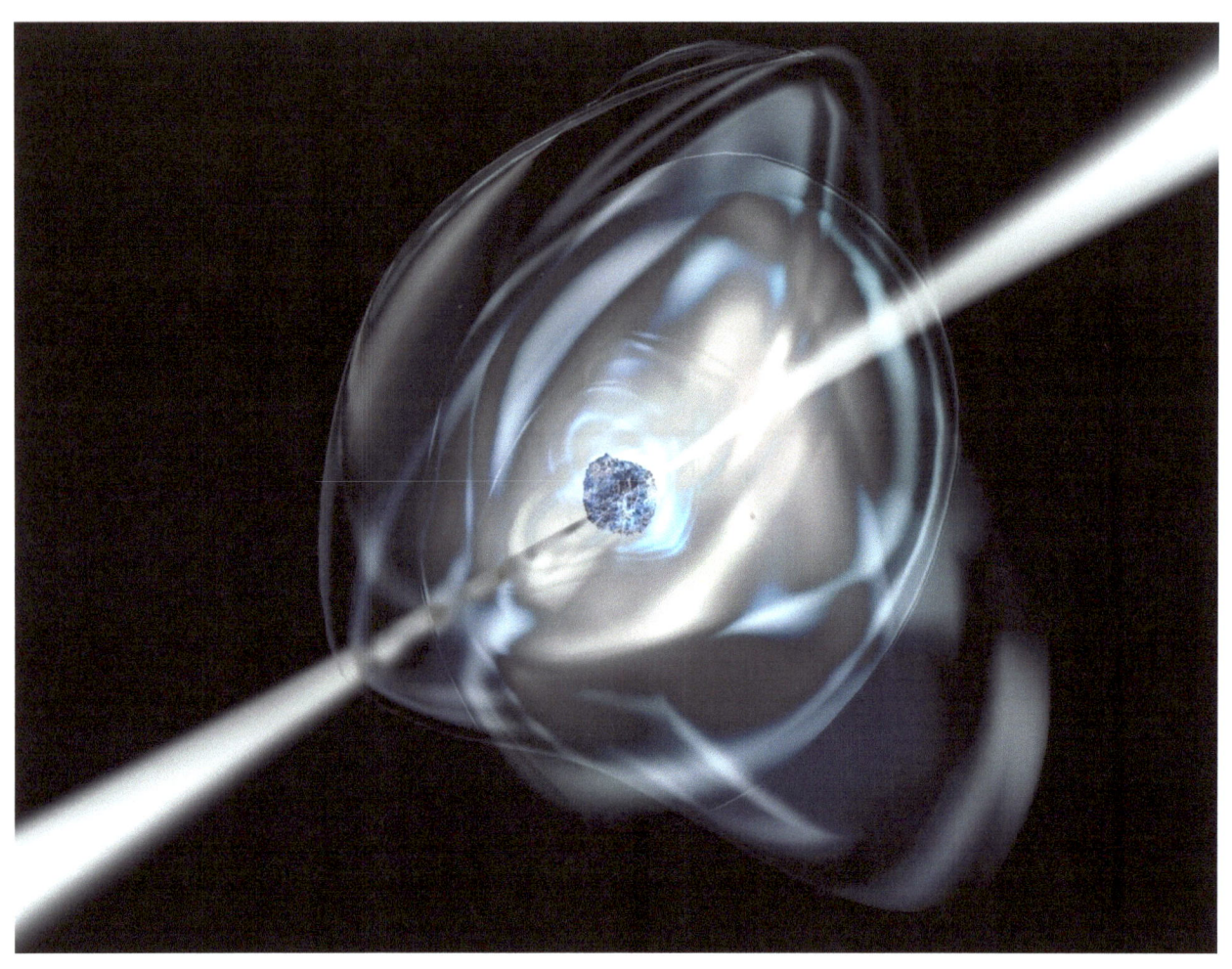

Magnetic
Neutron Star with huge magnetic fields

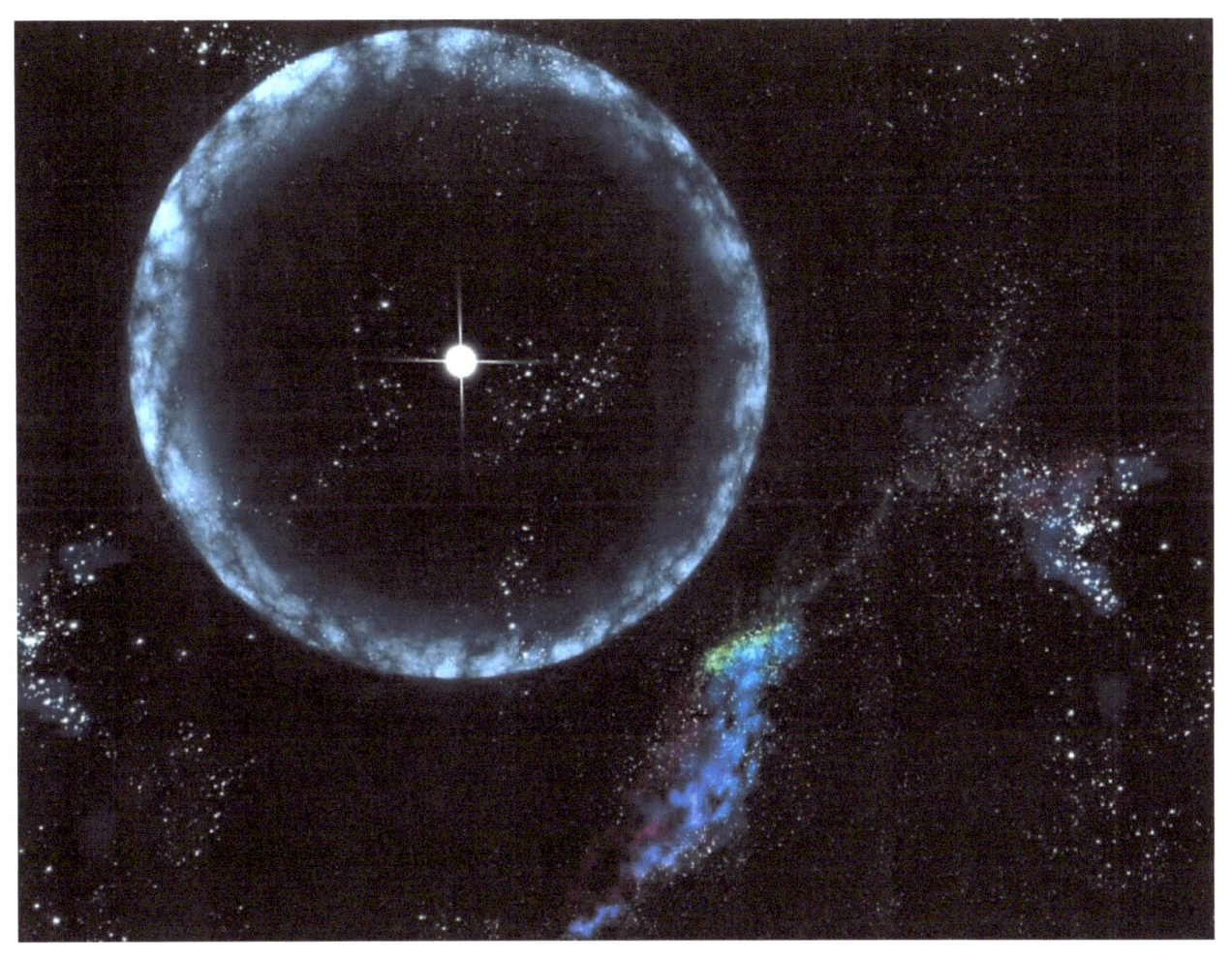

Density
Incredible compressed
neutron star

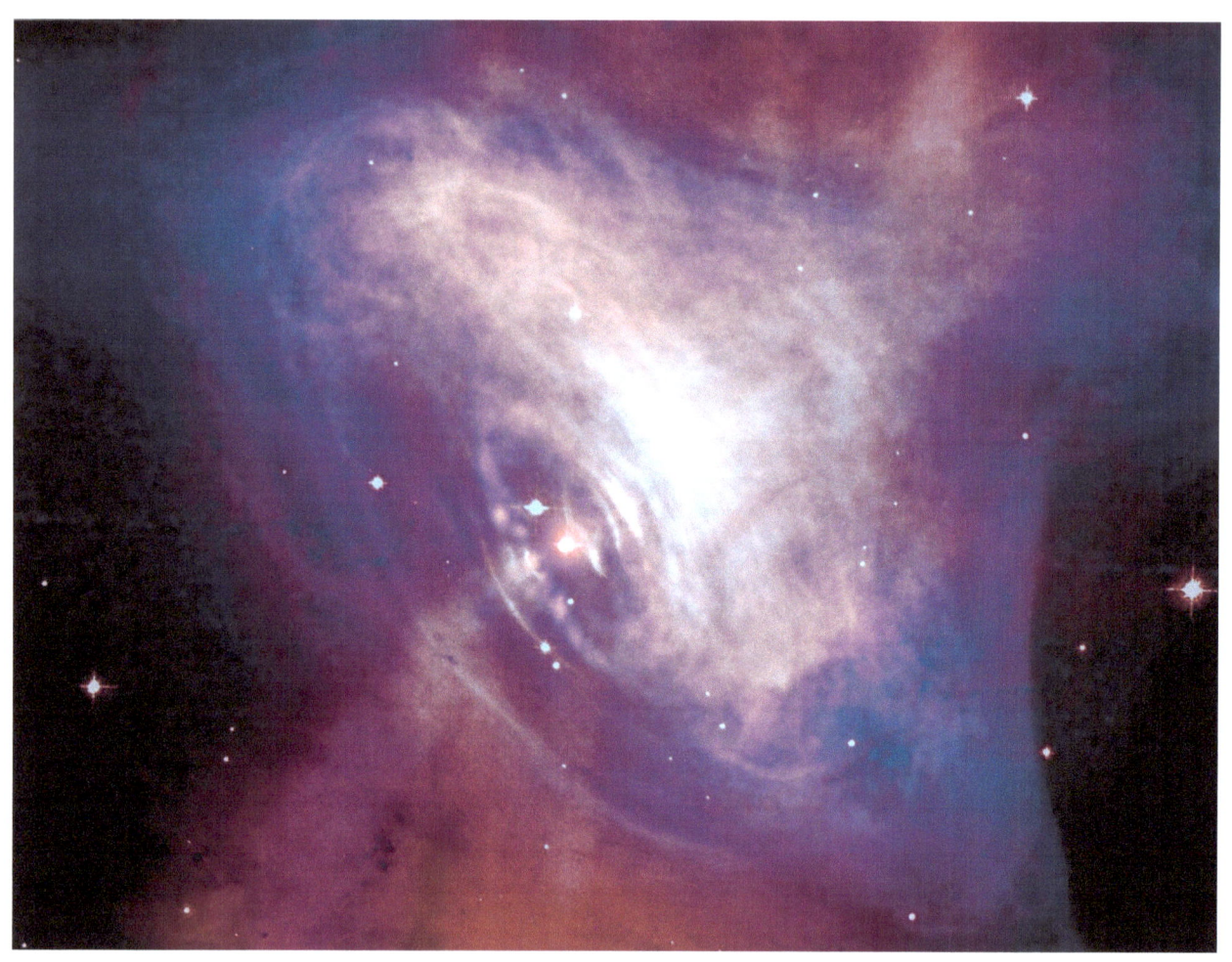

Transparency
Neutron star
in x-ray light

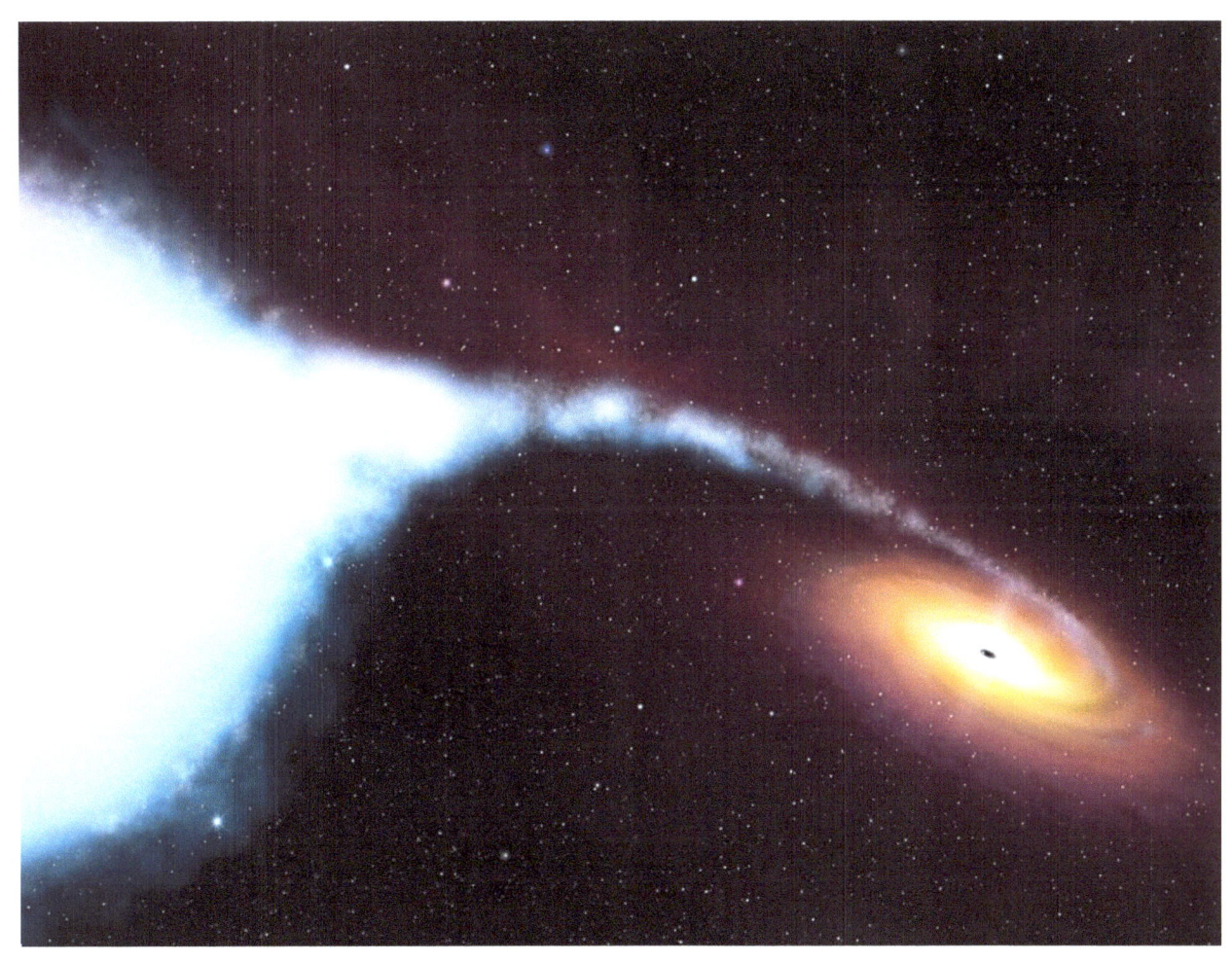

Attraction
Object being dispersed
by a black hole

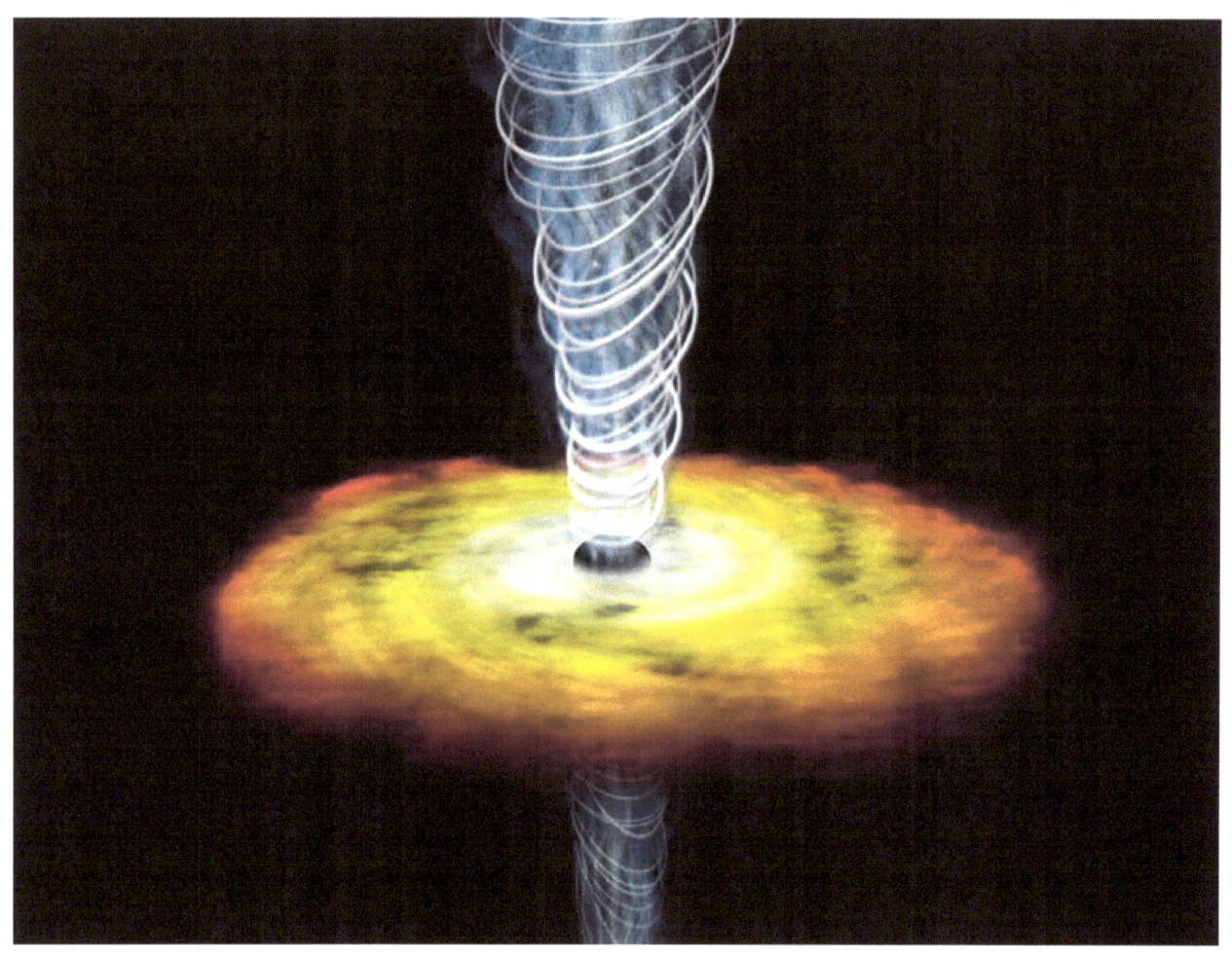

Quasar
Giant jets stream
out of the centre

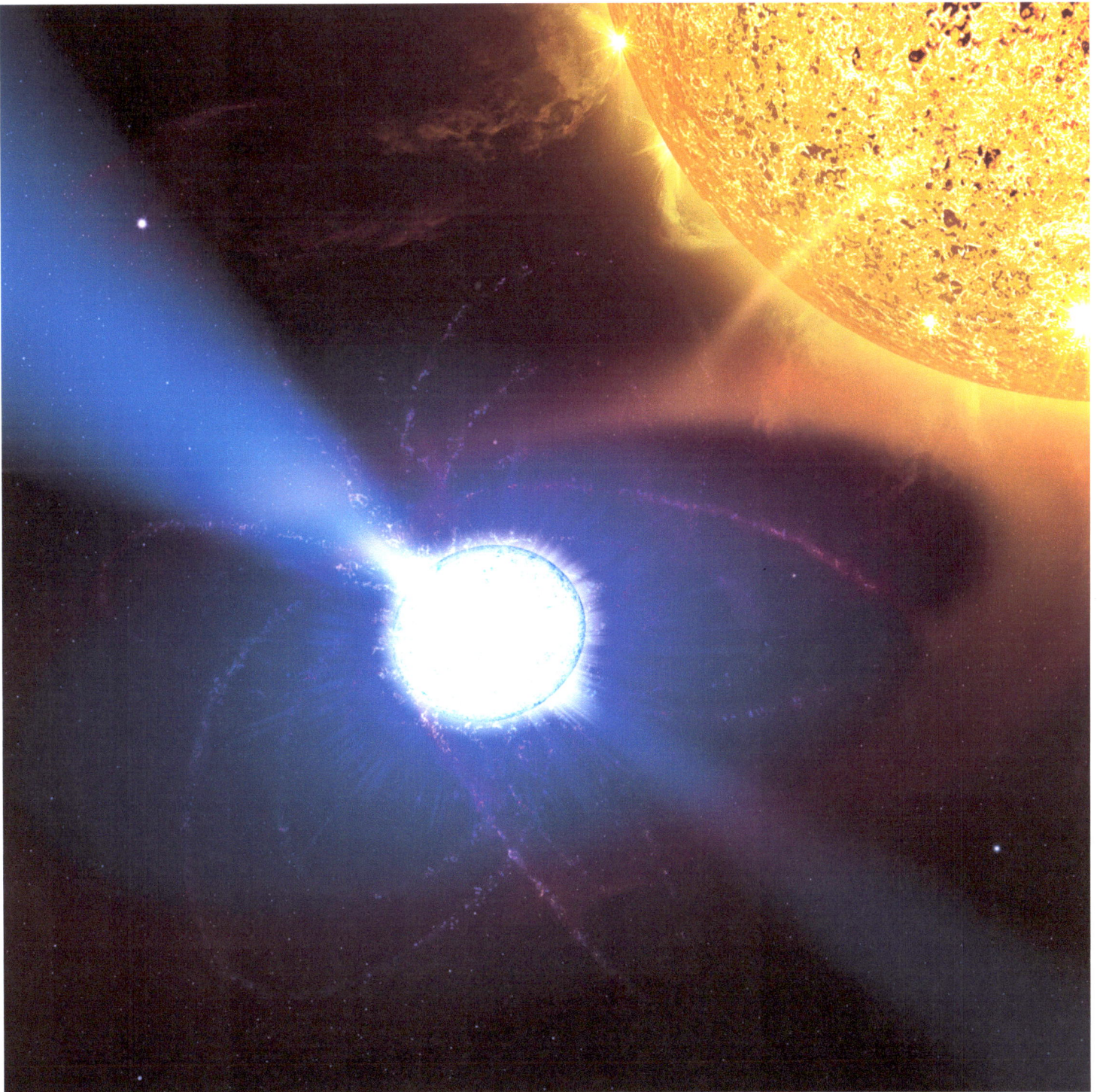

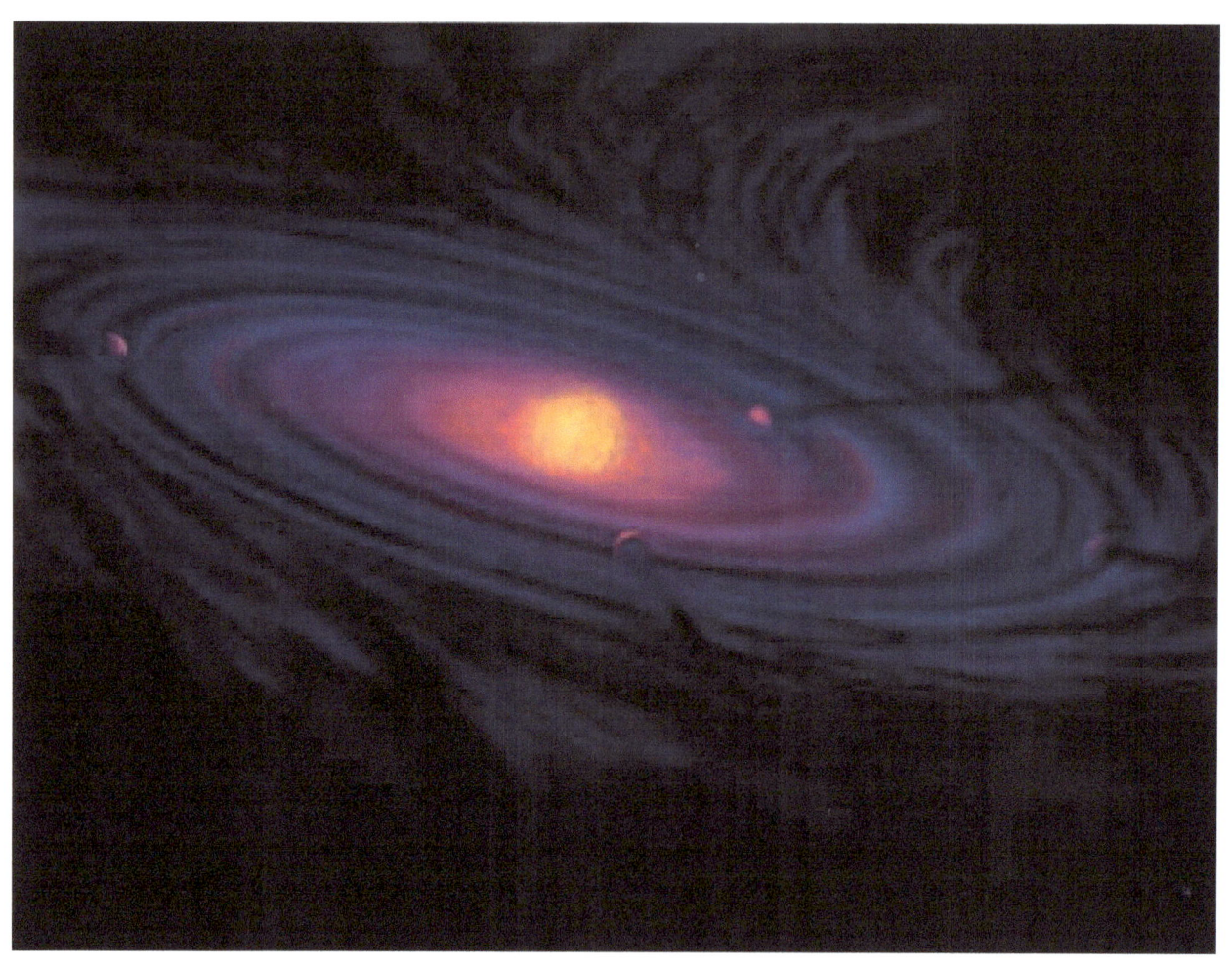

Formation
Origin of a
solar system

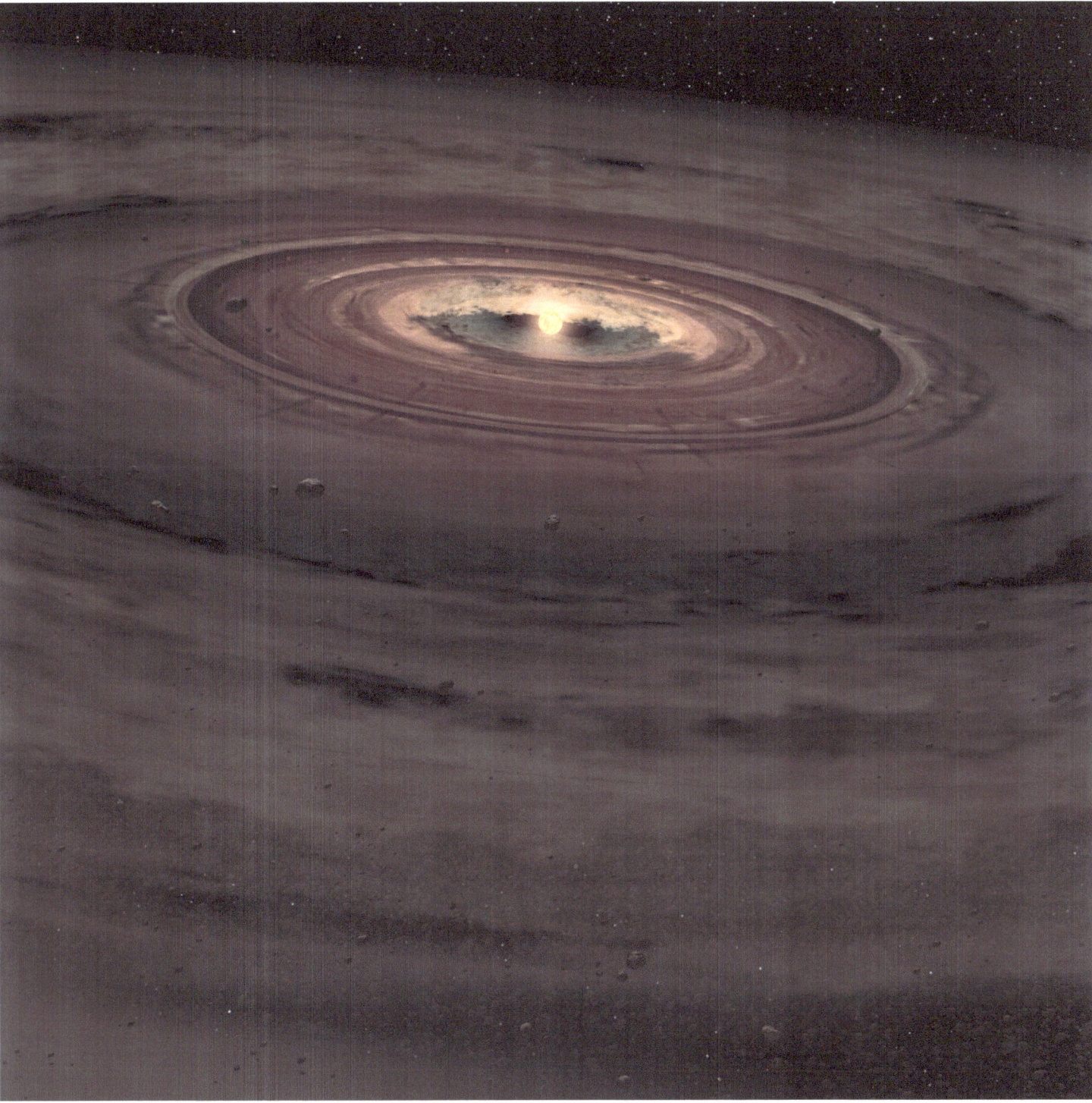

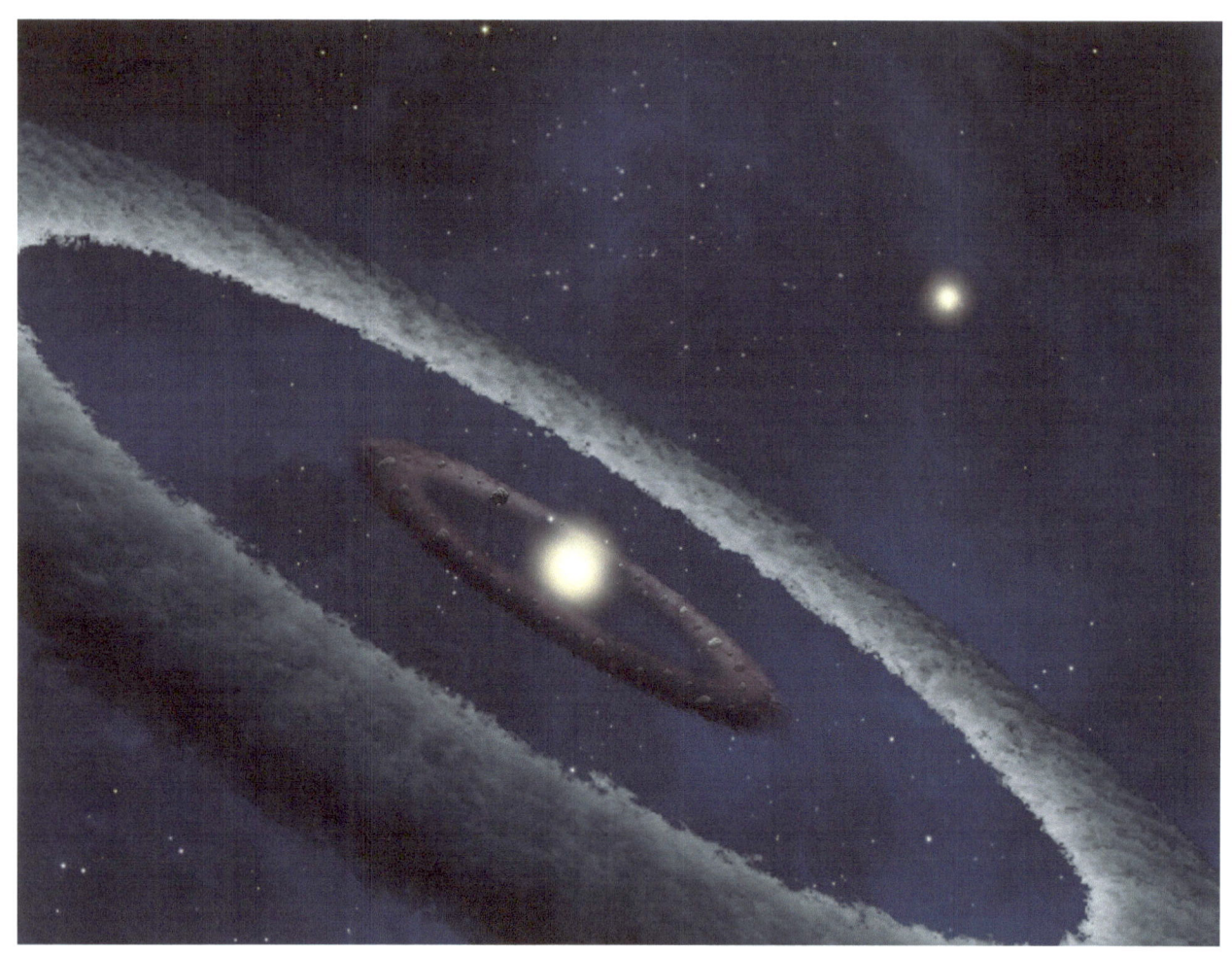

Compression
The disc became a
belt of rocks and planets

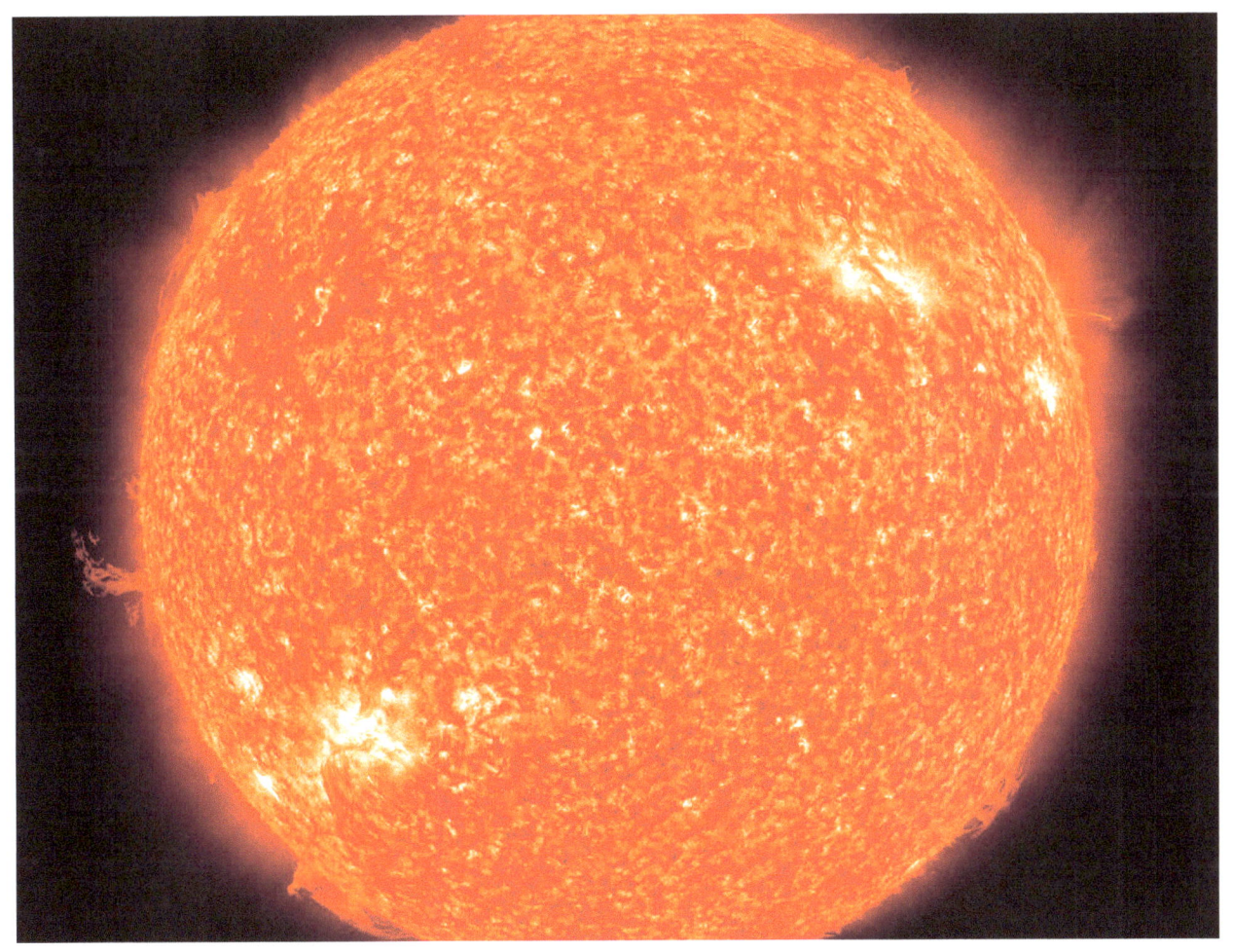

Caught Fire
The Sun as a central star
of the Solar System

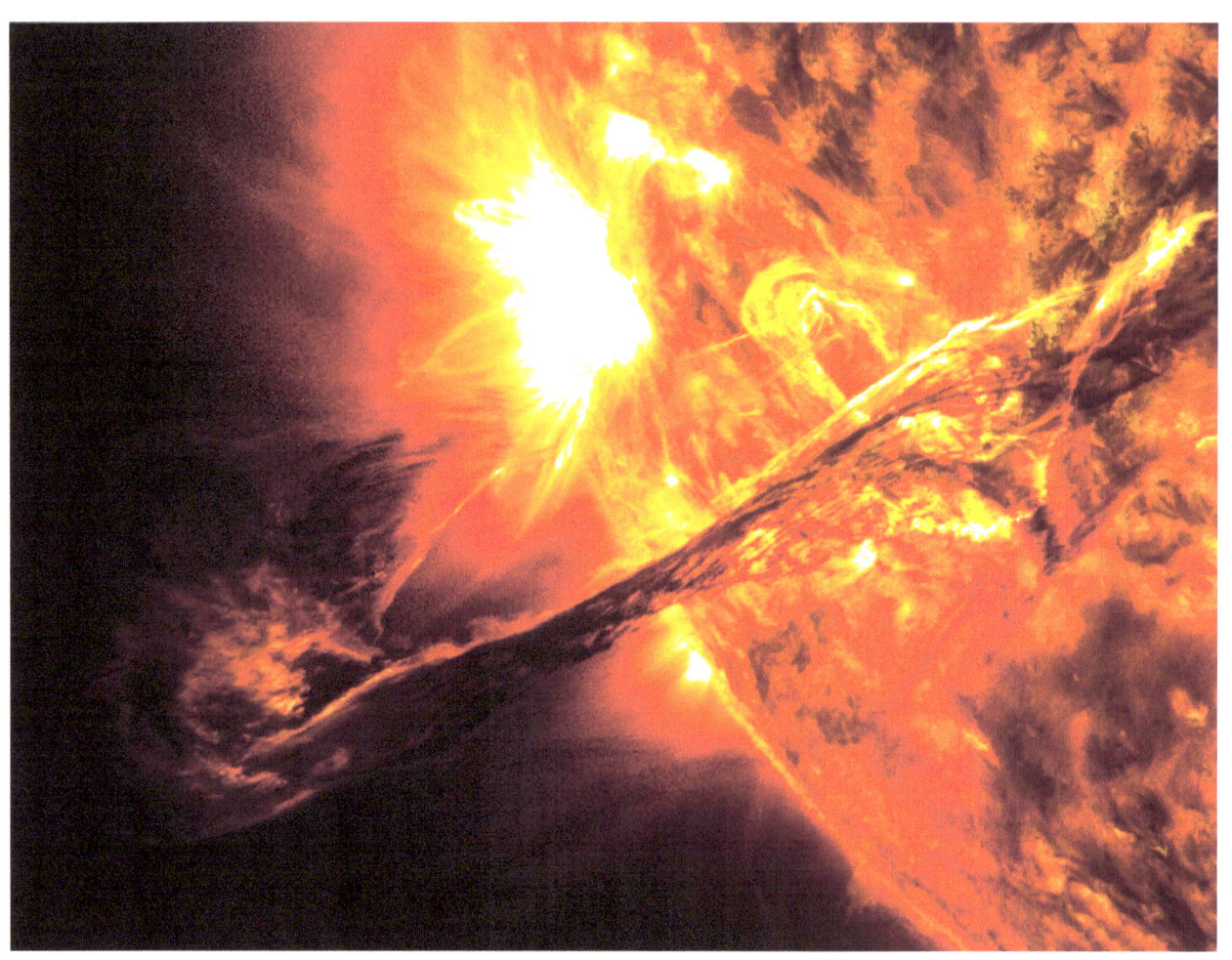

Solar Eruption

Huge eruptions hurtle
hot plasma into space

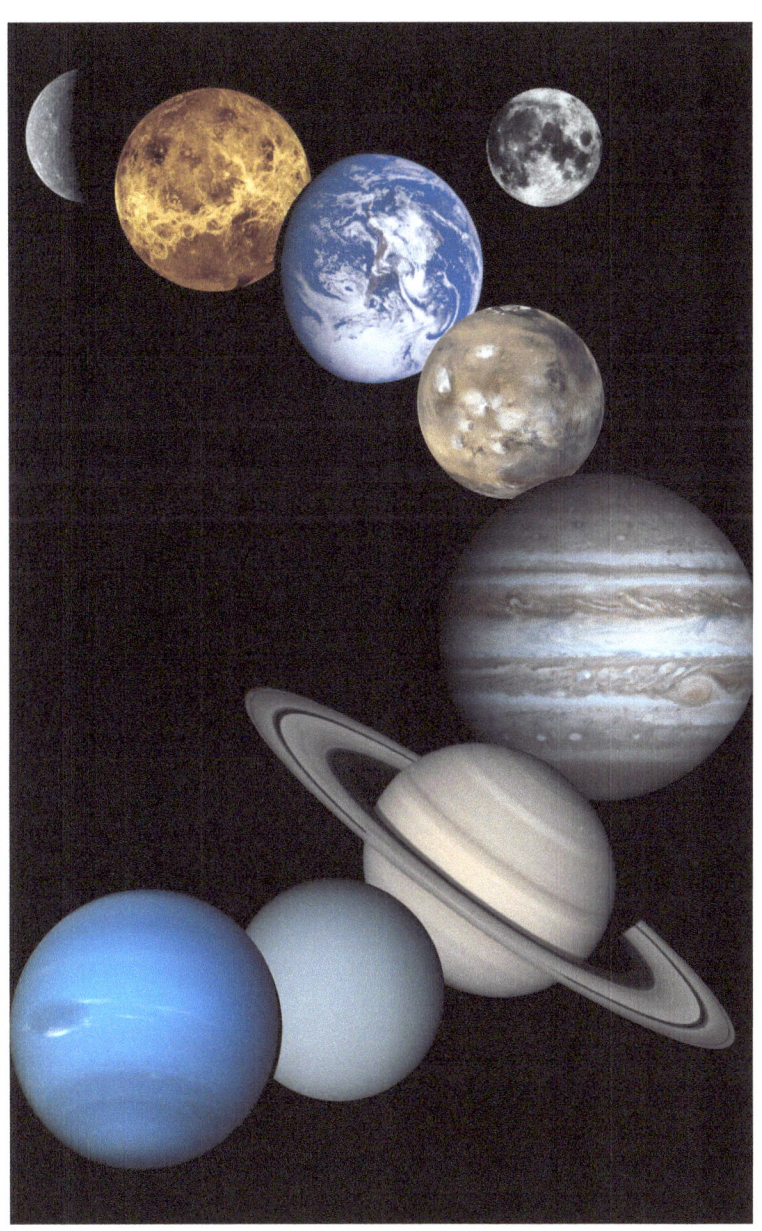

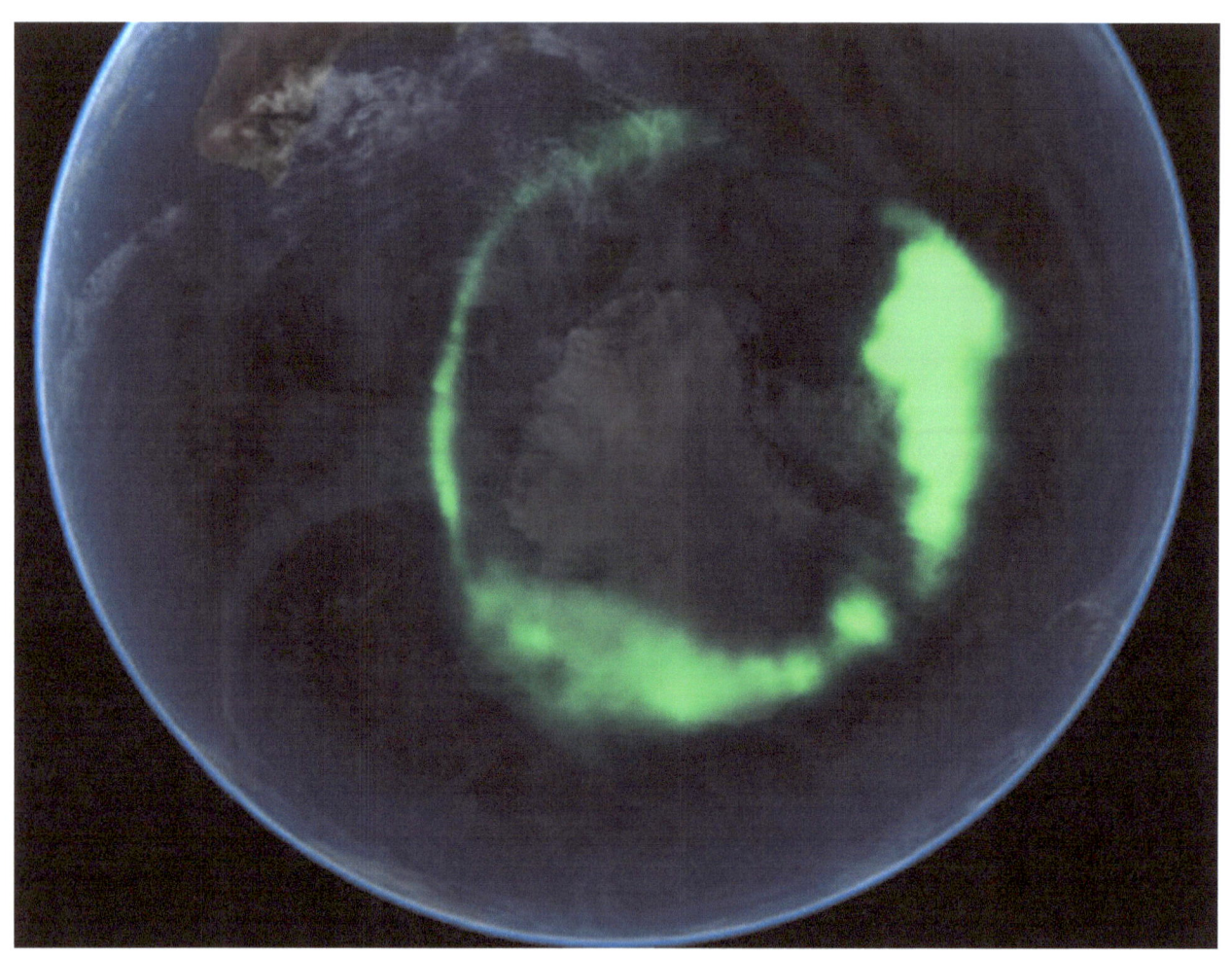

Protection Shield
Charged solar particles
enlightens the atmosphere

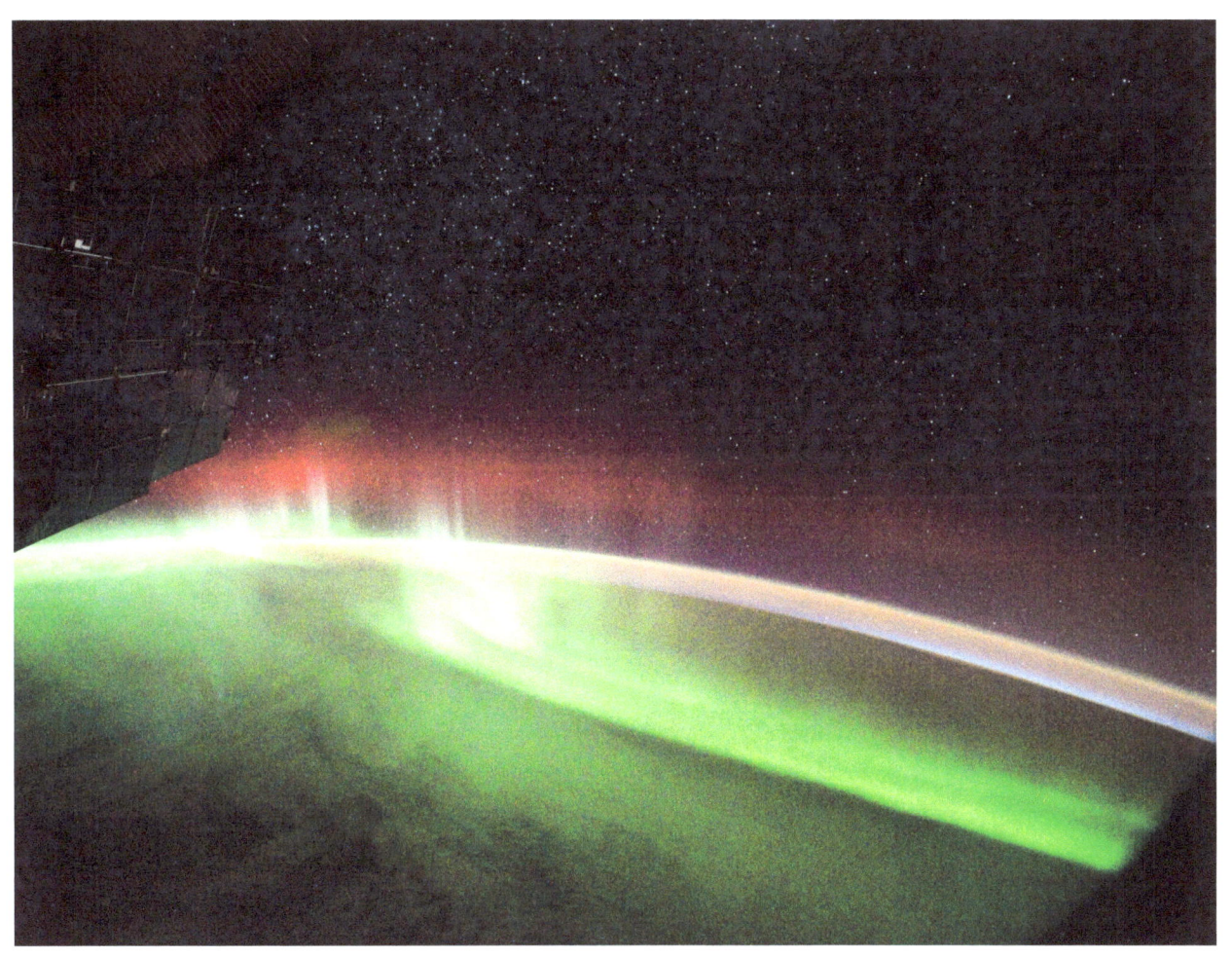

Polar Lights

Atmospherical light
induced by particles

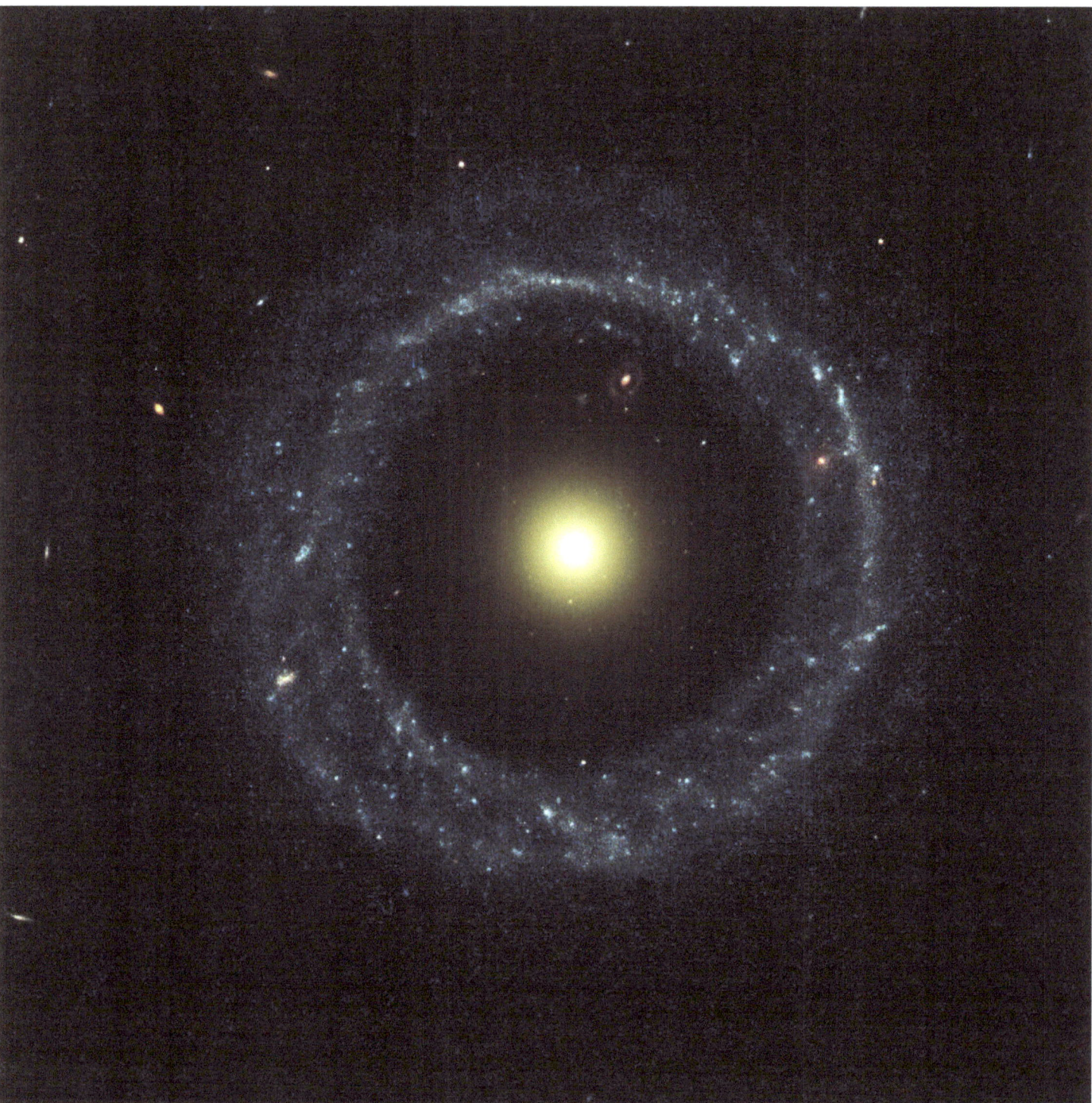

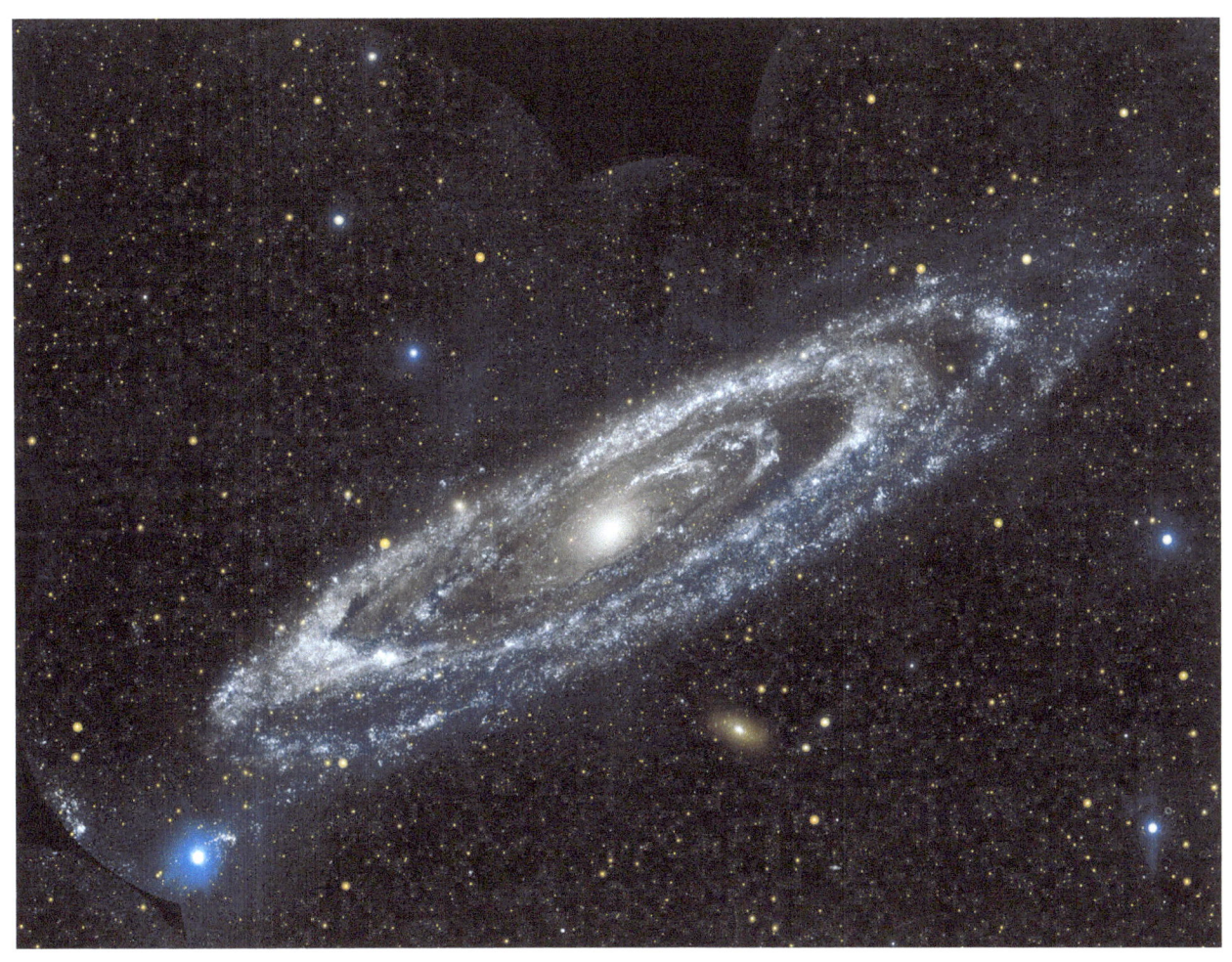

Islands of Worlds
A galaxy contains many many stars
Part of worlds

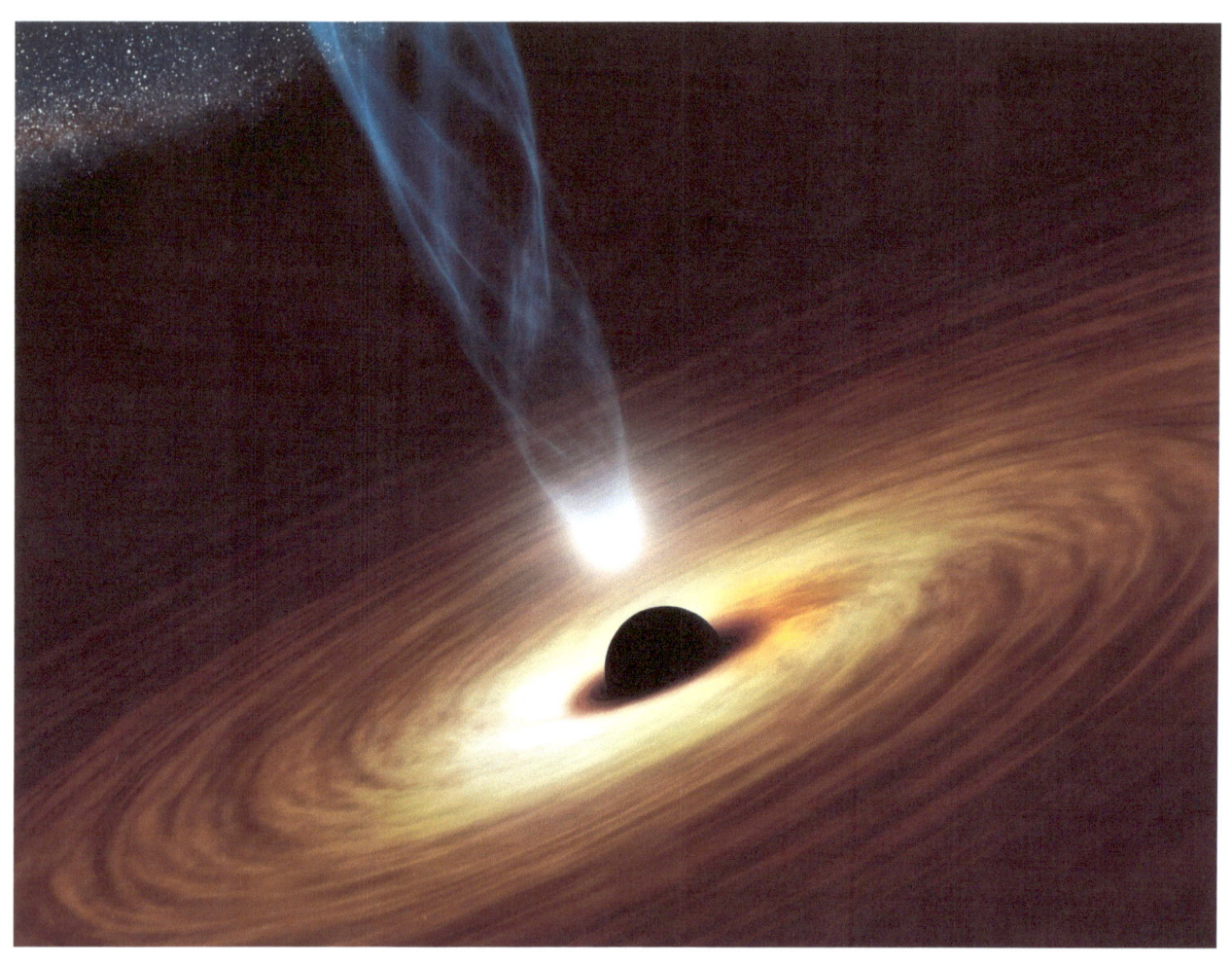

Too Dense

Black Hole in the center of a galaxy

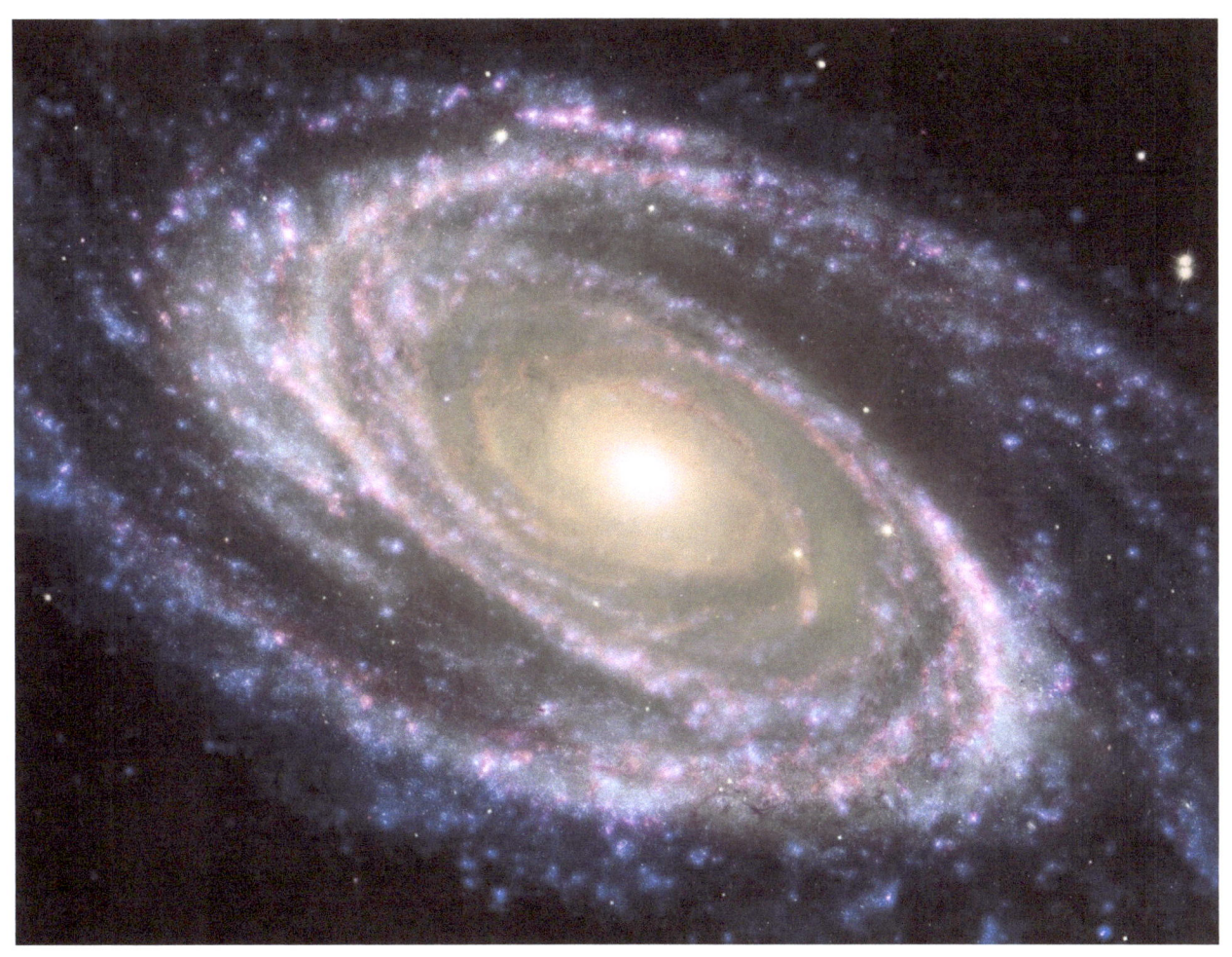

Our Galaxy
Milky Way - Galaxy with spiral arms

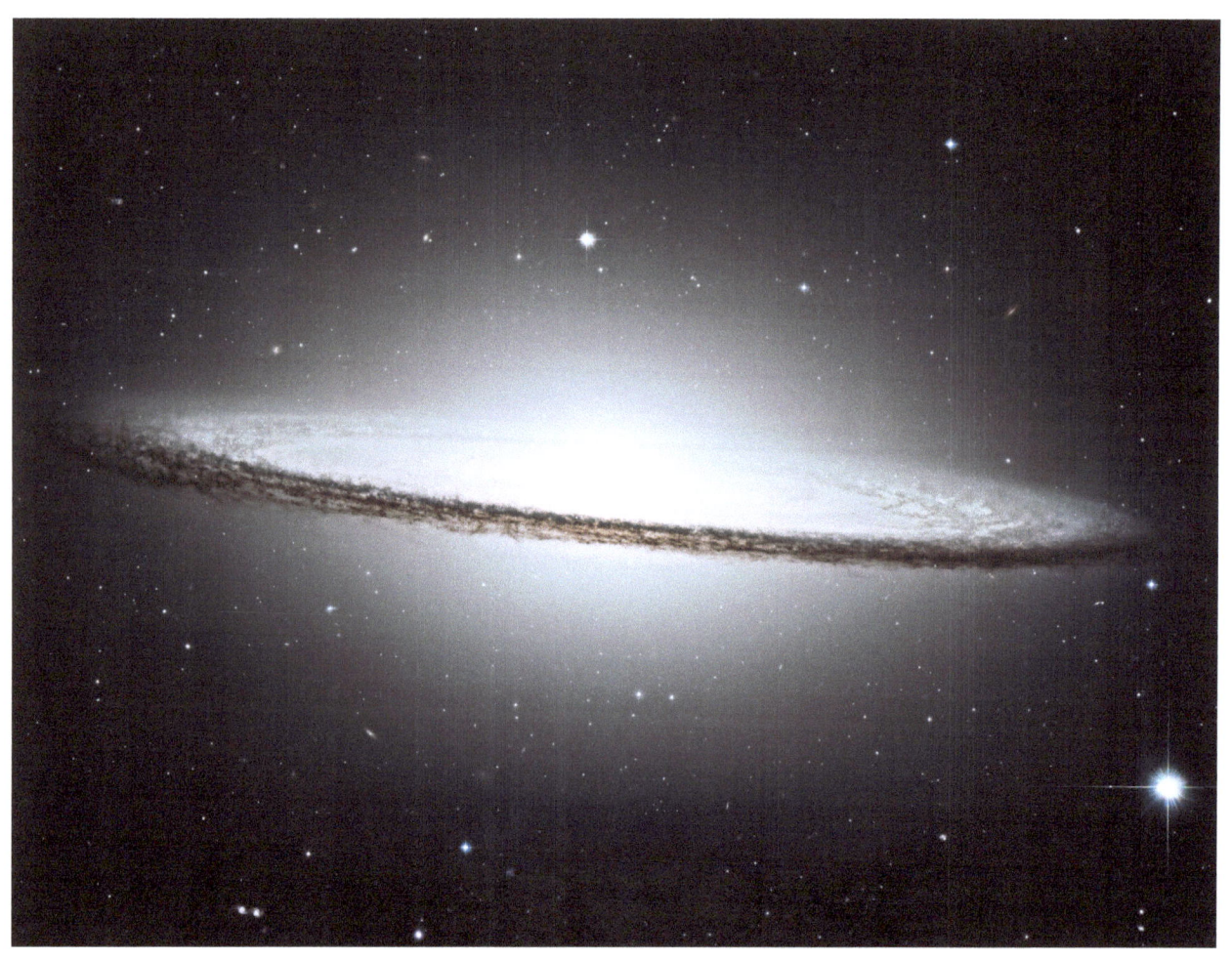

Interesting Edge
Galaxy with interesting edge
Sombrero Galaxy

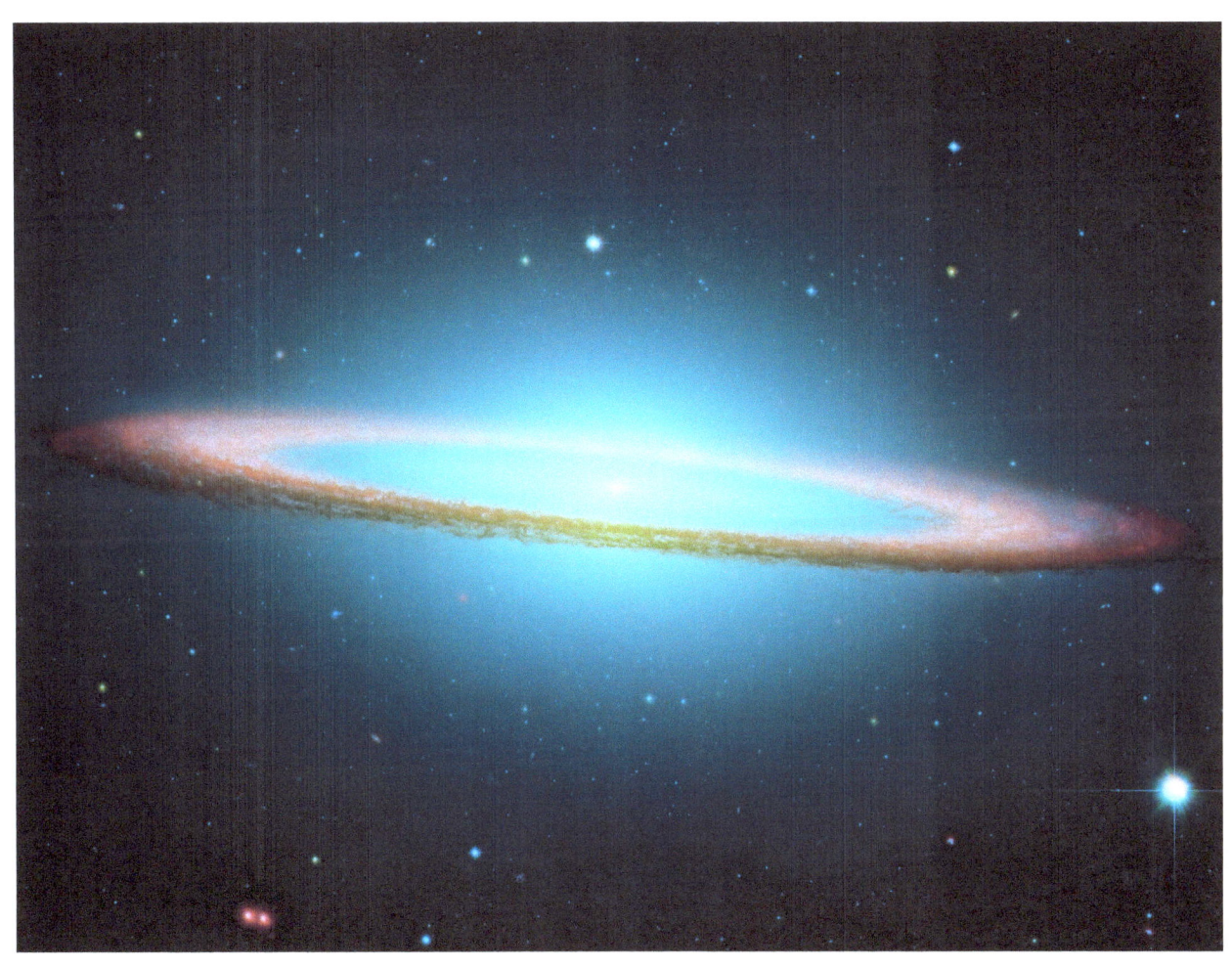

Heat Visible

Sombrero Galaxy in the
heat ray spectrum

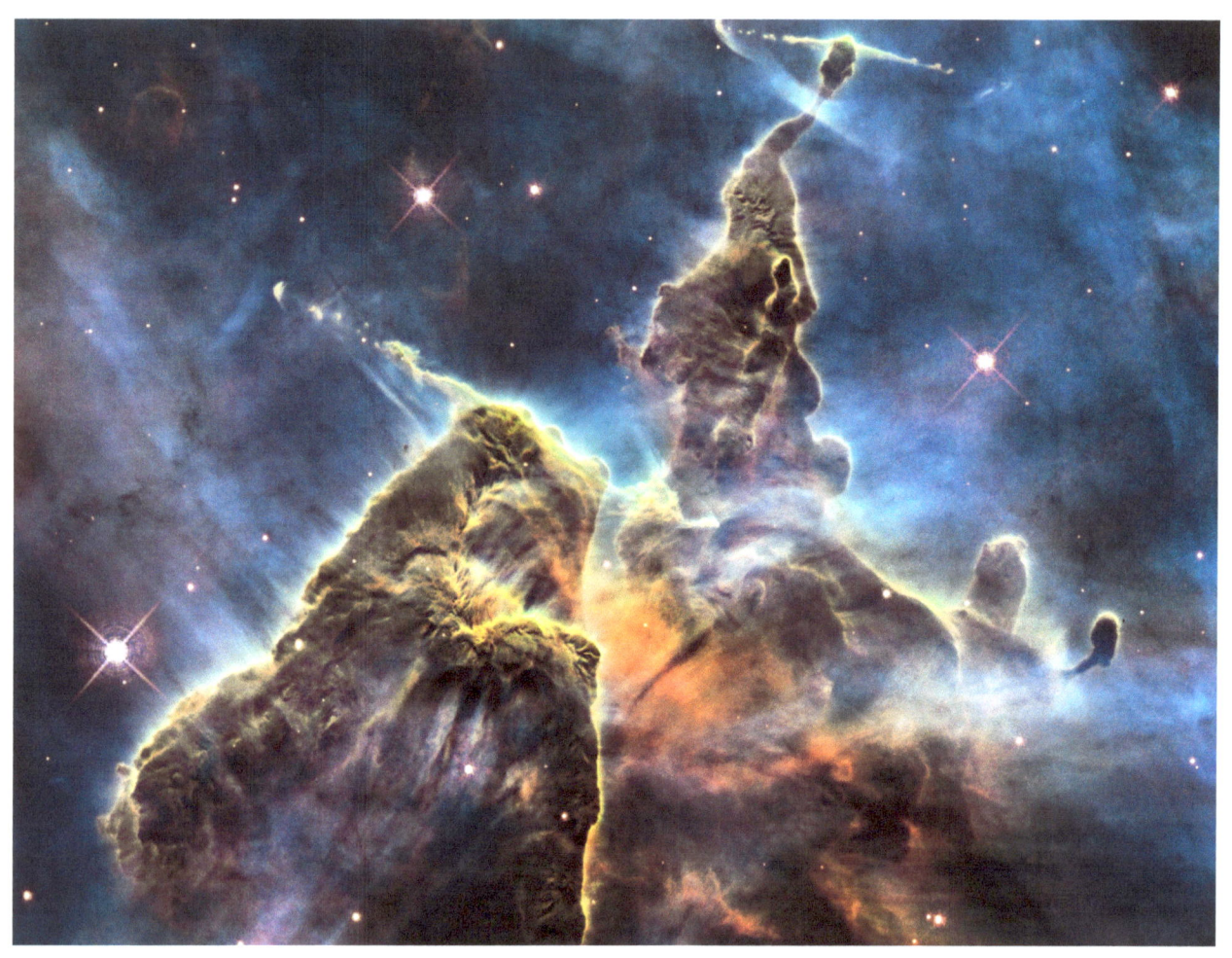

Star Formation

Star Formation regions - cradles of
new born stars

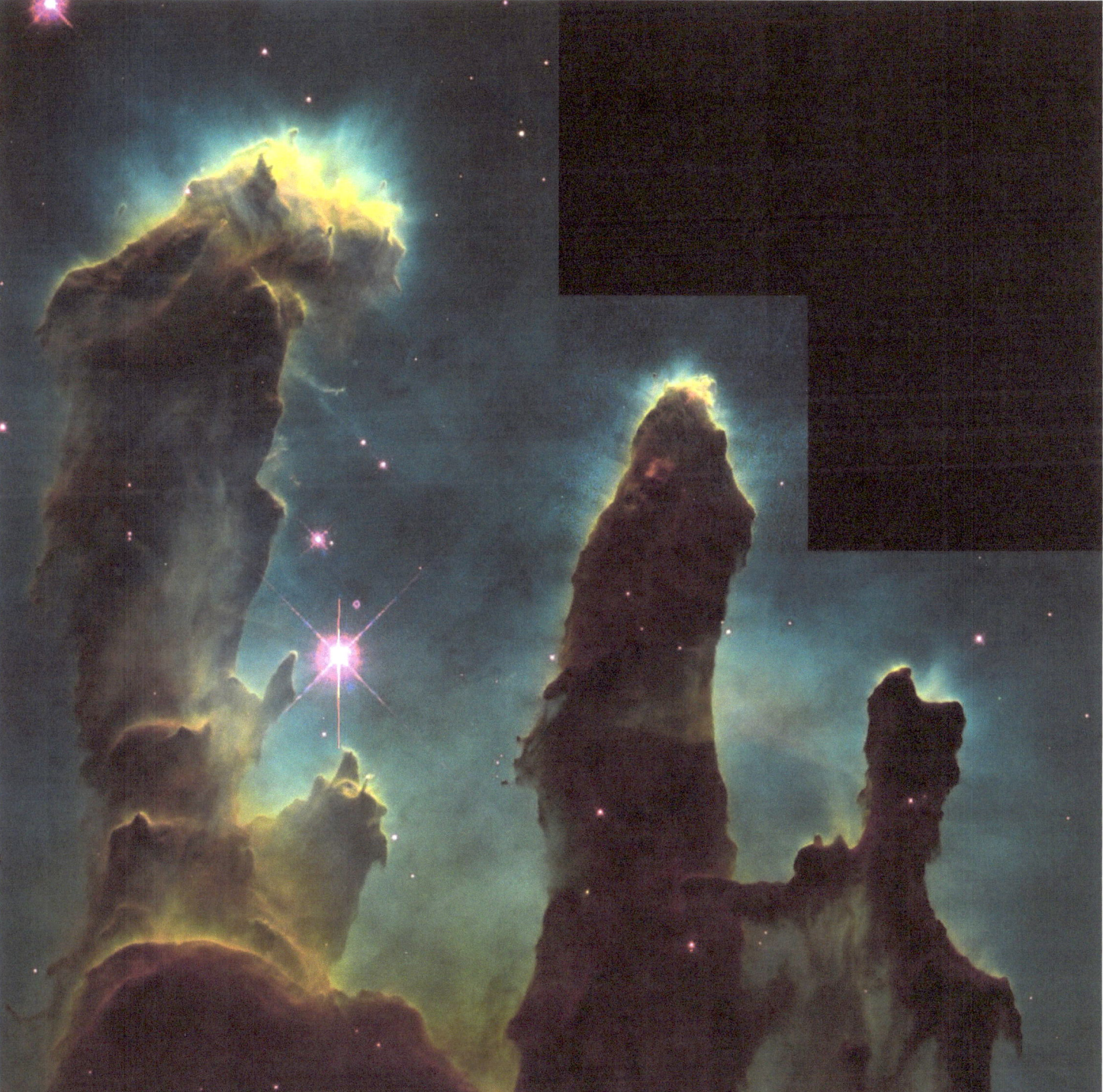

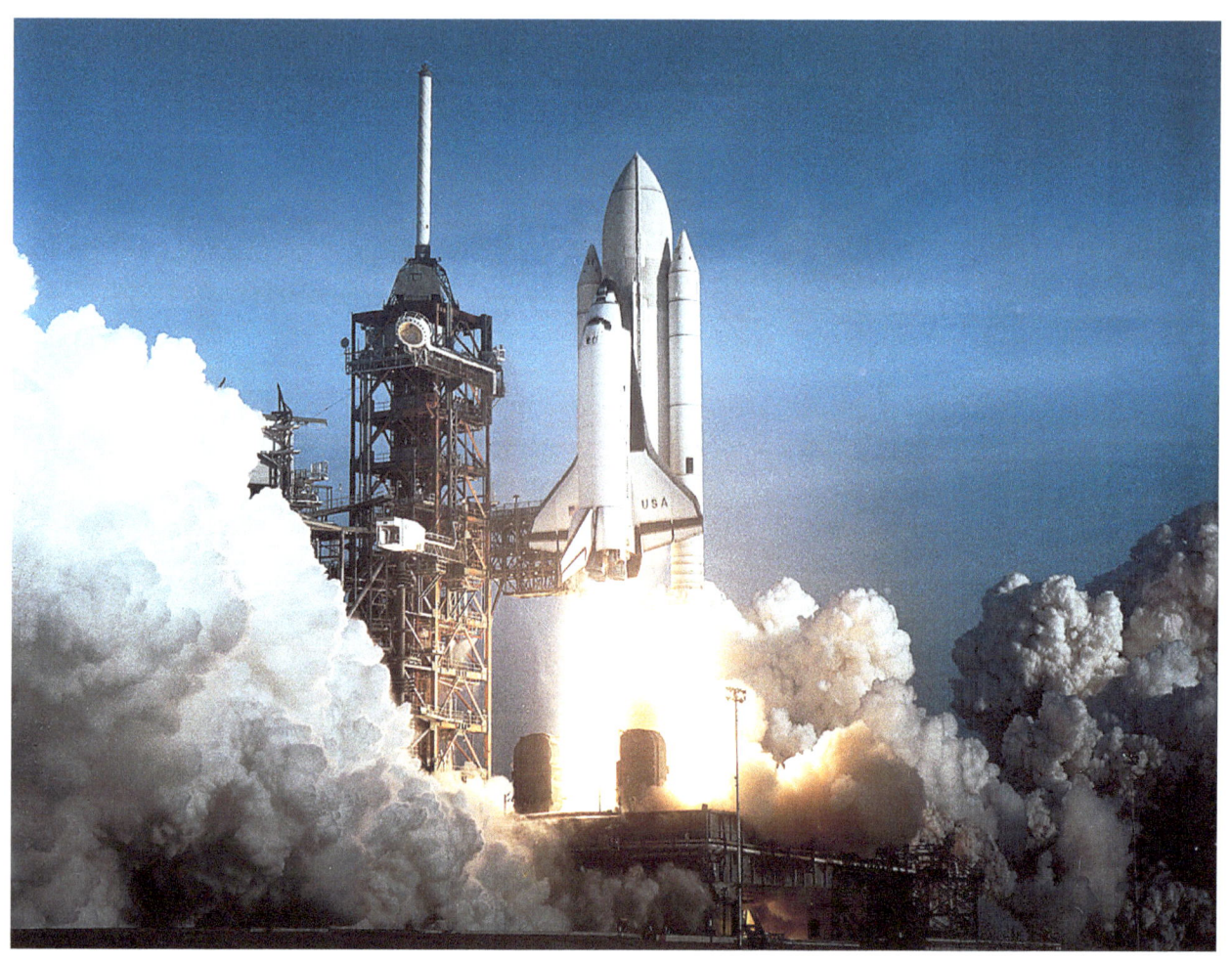

Break Free
Space Shuttle - Doorway into Space

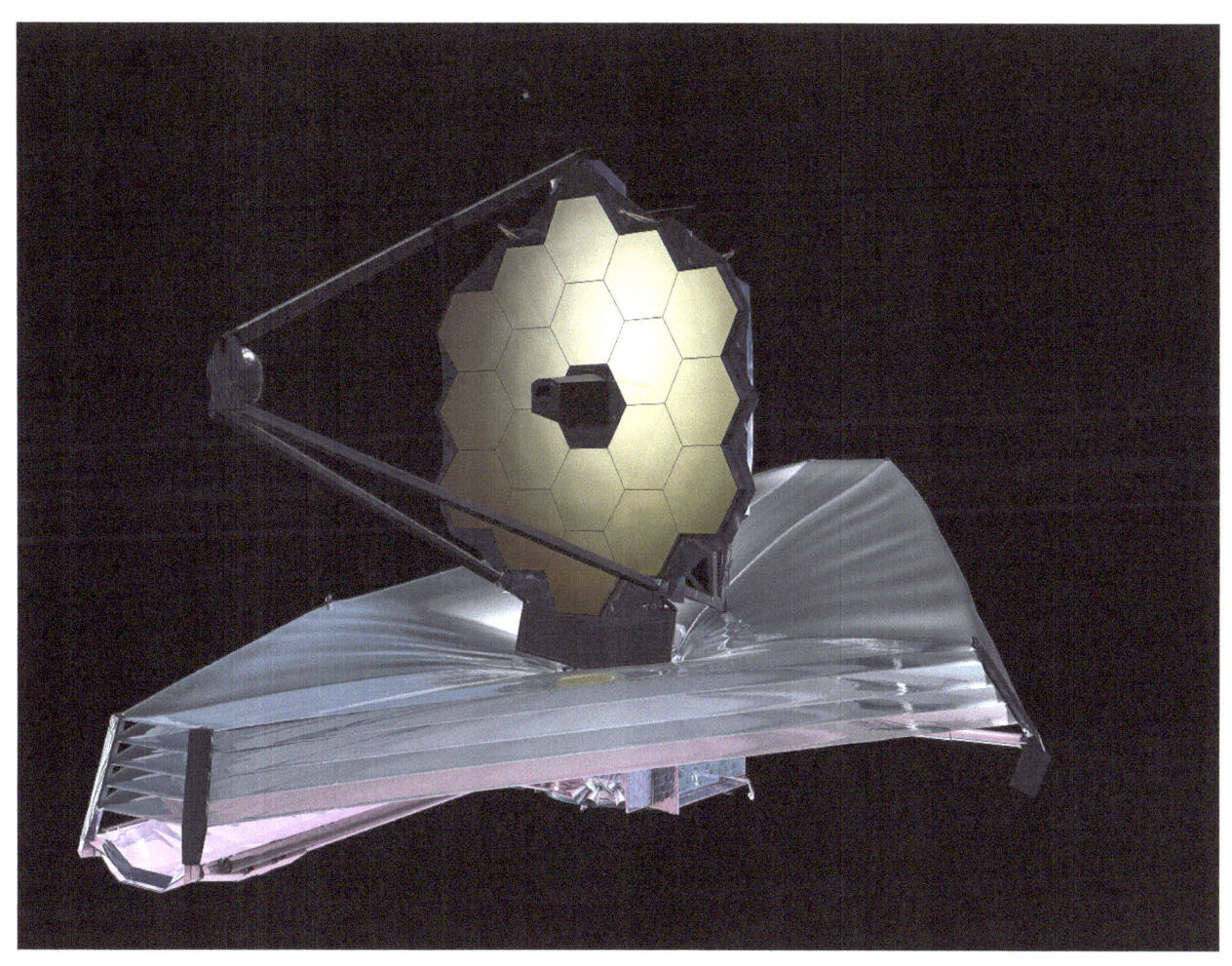

Window Into Space
James Webb Telescope
Space based reflector telescope

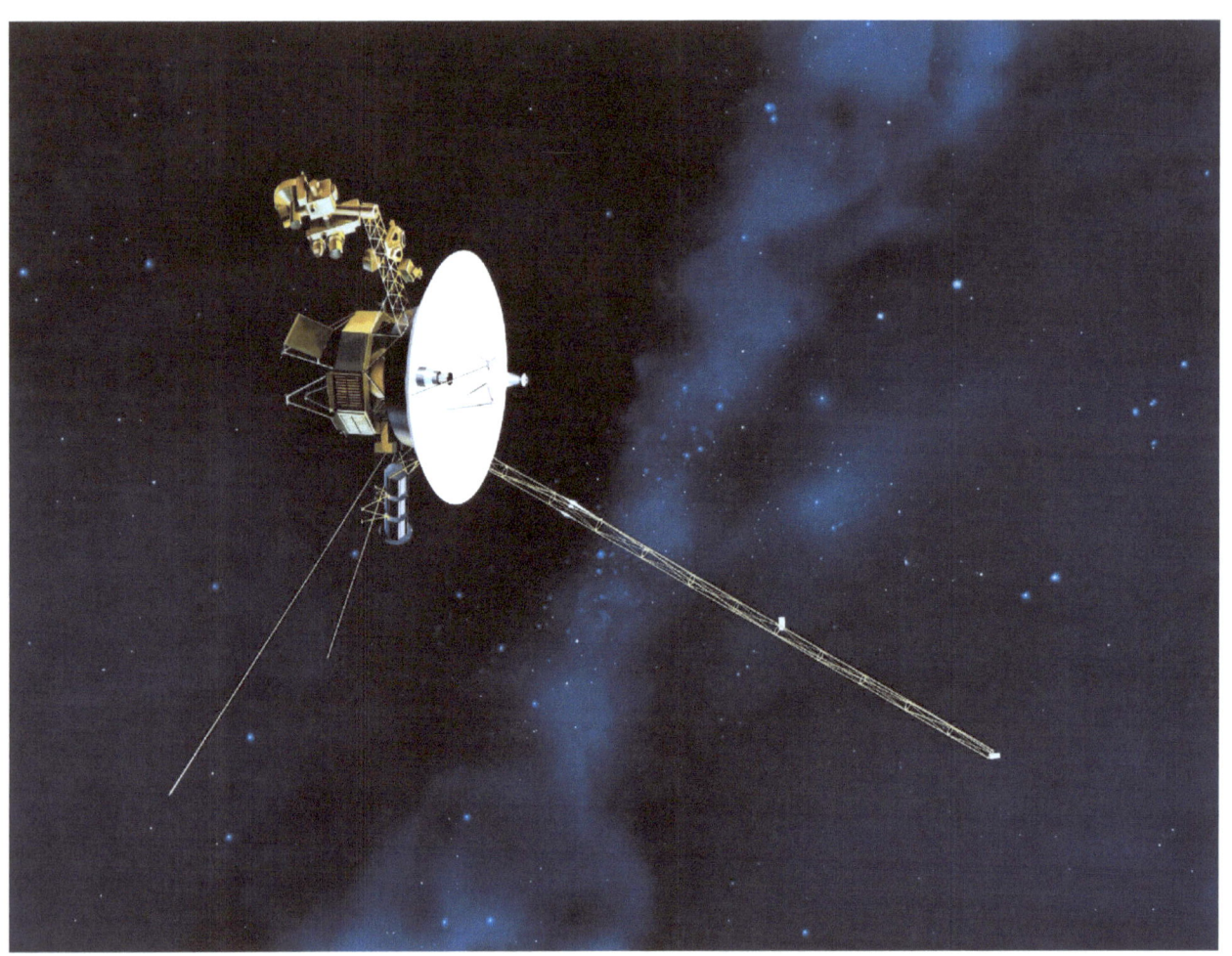

First Messenger
Space Probe Voyager
Message for good

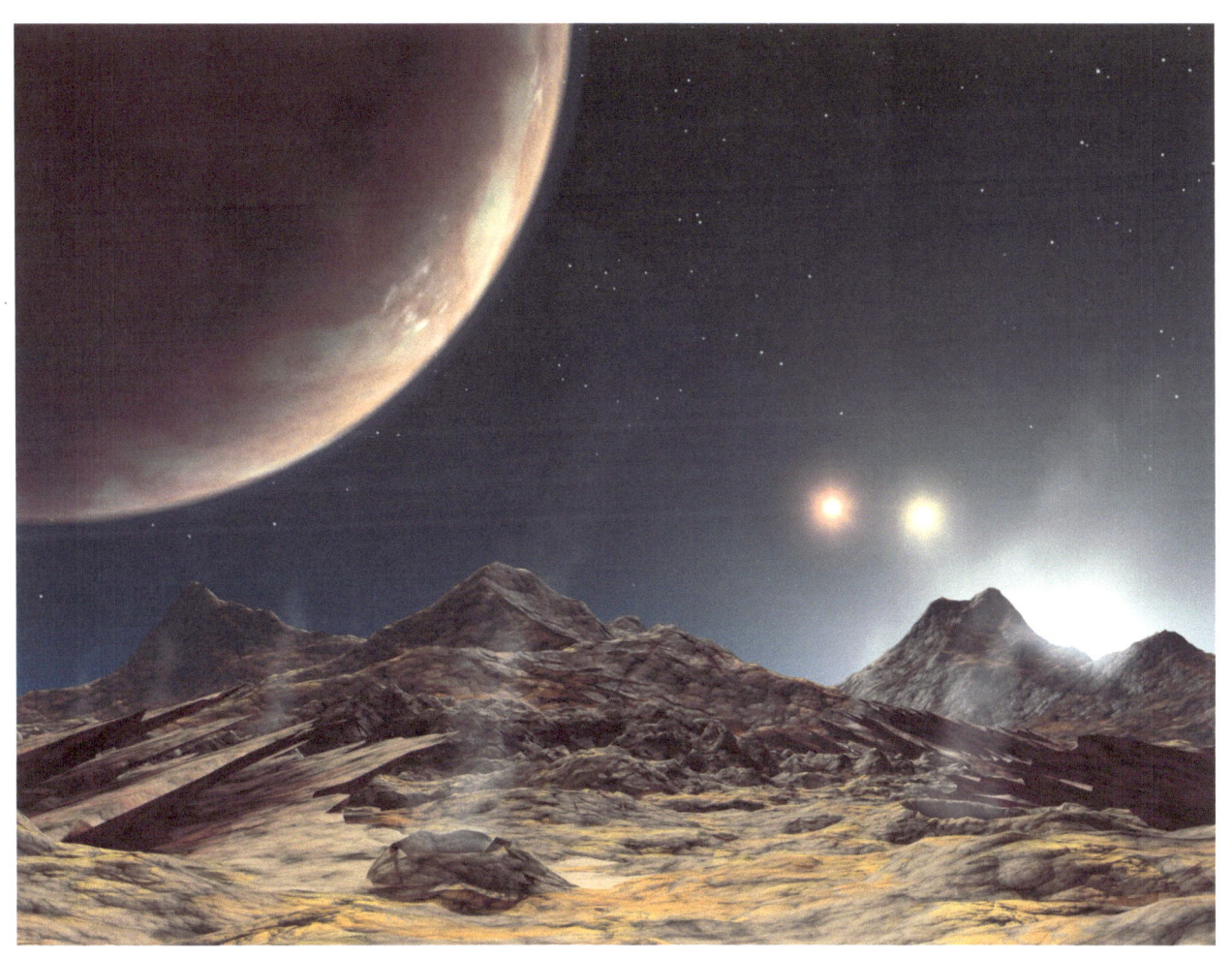

Distant Worlds

Sunrise with three stars in a
different world

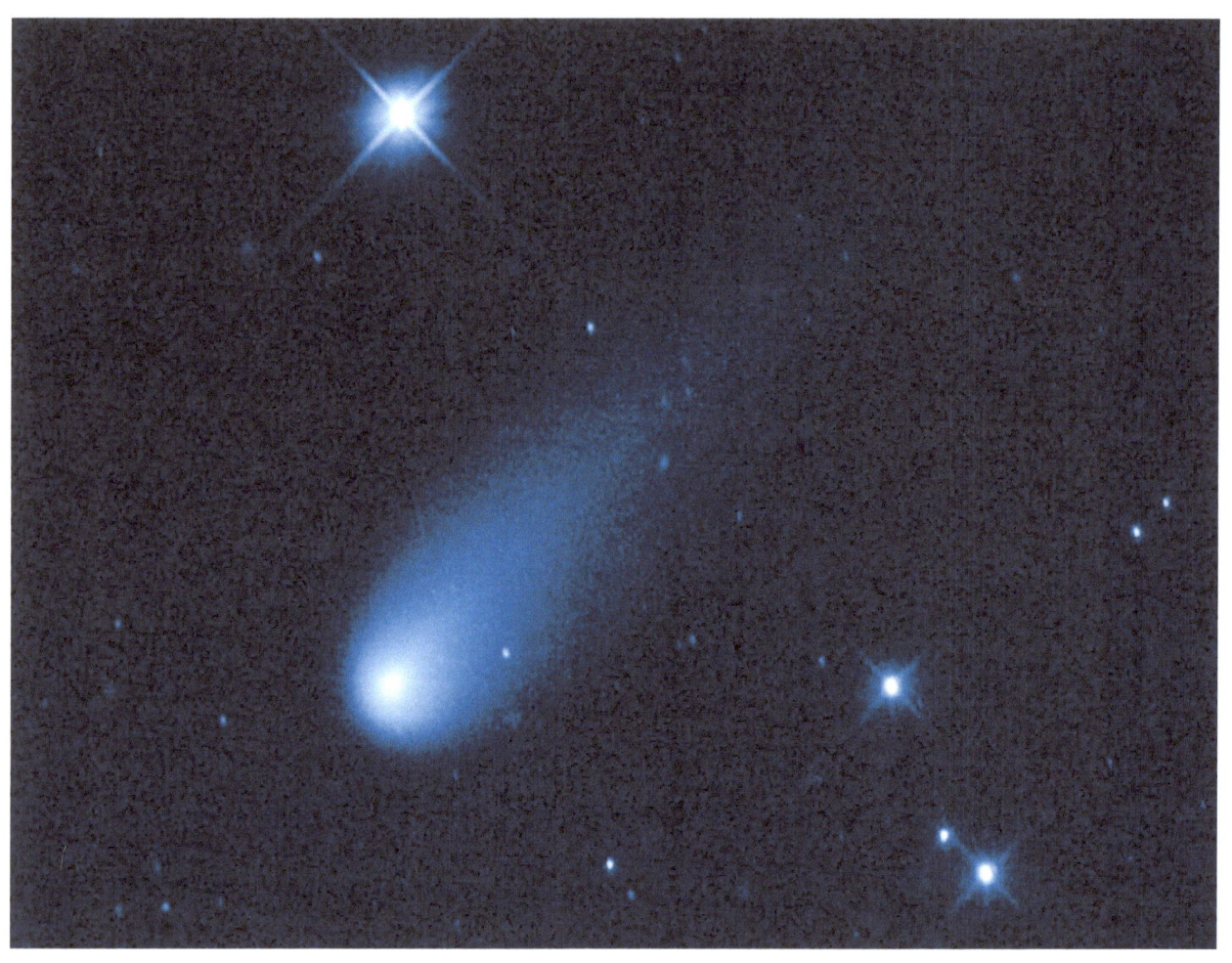

Comet ISON
Comets - Carrier from the
Solar System

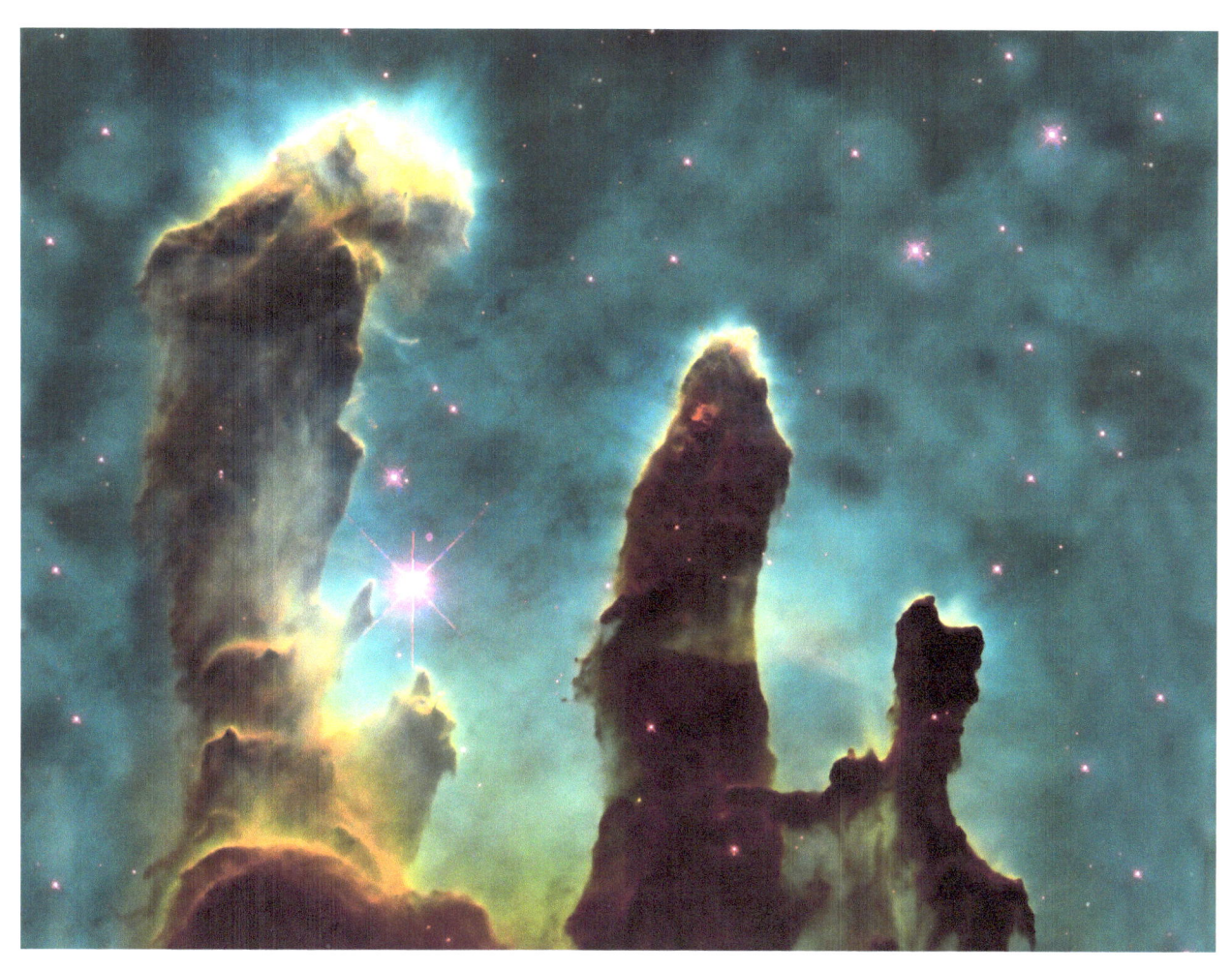

Welcome Back

www.ingramcontent.com/pod-product-compliance
Lightning Source LLC
Chambersburg PA
CBHW051111180526
45172CB00002B/870

*   9   7   8   1   2   9   1   6   3   4   6   1   7   *